Manager's Pocket Guide to
Interviewing and Hiring Top Performers

Sarah J. Ennis

D1559992

HRD Press, Inc.

Published by:

    Human Resource Development Press, Inc.
    22 Amherst Road
    Amherst, MA 01002
    (800) 822-2801 (U.S. and Canada)
    (413) 253-3488
    (413) 253-3490 (fax)
    http://www.hrdpress.com

ISBN 0-87425-664-X

Production services by Jean Miller
Editorial services by Sally Farnham
Cover design by Eileen Klockars

Acknowledgements

To Todd McDonald for his assistance in getting this project going to begin with, and his invaluable help in its completion.

To my family for their constant love and support.

To my business colleagues and clients from whom I learn every day.

Table of Contents

Introduction

Today's tight labor market is forcing organizations to maximize the time they spend attracting and keeping top performers. Organizations that can attract, inspire, and retain top performers are in the position to beat out their competition. This is true both in market share and being able to draw outstanding employees.

This book is for individuals with training responsibilities who are looking for tools to help their managers, supervisors, and/or team leaders interview, hire, and retain top performers. If you or someone in your hiring system has limited experience in interviewing and hiring, this book will help you and your organization be more proficient in hiring practices.

Chapter One:
The Importance of Hiring Right

Chapter Objectives

This chapter covers strategies to help you:

- ➢ Understand the high cost of employee turnover.
- ➢ Analyze the effects of poor employee placement.
- ➢ Know what a good hire means to an organization.
- ➢ Use four strategies for hiring right.
- ➢ Write effective job descriptions.

In today's competitive job market, hiring the right person for the job is critical for success. There are many variables that can have a major impact on hiring:

- Time constraints that force hasty decisions

- Informal or incomplete hiring process

- Unstructured interviews

- Novice or improperly trained interviewers

- Decisions based on intuition, assumptions, snap judgments, and gut feelings

Needless to say, these pitfalls create an unreliable system on which to base important hiring decisions that can have lasting effects on your organization.

High Cost of Turnover

It is a well-known fact that it is more costly to attract and gain new customers than it is to keep existing customers. The same holds true for recruiting and hiring new employees. It is less expensive to retain employees than it is to hire new ones. Depending on the industry and the position being filled, the hiring process can cost as much as 30 to 100 percent of the new hire's annual salary. In situations where a structured hiring system is absent or an extensive search is required for key positions, it can cost even more.

The total cost of employee turnover includes:

- Recruiting expenditures

- Time to screen and interview candidates multiplied by the number of people involved

- Time and resources required to train the new employee

- Loss of productivity due to the learning curve of the new hire

- Loss of productivity from the people taking time from their regular duties while all of this is taking place

During this turnover time, your organization might also be less productive because of a vacant position. This could mean losing customers and business during the transition.

A great deal of employee turnover occurs because of mismatching the job with the person or hiring decisions not firmly established in facts. This is not to say that the interviewing process can be foolproof. It is and always will be an imperfect science. You can, however, do a great deal to decrease the subjective nature of hiring to secure the odds in your favor.

Take a moment to brainstorm all of the specific costs you sustain during one instance of employee turnover. List the sources of expense and the approximate amount of each one to see what turnover means to you and your organization. The list on page 4 has been started for you. Complete it by adding any other expenses incurred by your organization due to turnover.

Turnover Costs Worksheet

Source	Expense
1. Recruiting costs/advertising	$
2. Time to screen applicants.	$
3. Time to interview applicants.	$
4. Time and resources to train new person.	$
5. Loss of productivity to learning curve.	$
6. Loss of productivity of others who "pick up the slack" in the transition.	$
7. Moving costs to relocate new hire	$
8.	$
9.	$
10.	$
11.	$
12.	$
Total Cost for One Employee Turnover =	$

How Successful Can Your Organization Be?

A great many factors go into making a successful organization. However, the key to the business formula that you've established is your people. Hiring the right people for the right positions can catapult you to success. If you do not take the time or use the best tools in your hiring process, you could be hurting your organization more than you know.

Think about a person in your organization who should not be in the position that he or she is in, for whatever reason. Analyze some of the short- and long-term ramifications of this situation by completing the chart on the following pages. Specify how each situation affects the strength of your organization.

If you were able to respond to one or more of the elements in this chart, think how many times this may be repeating itself already in your organization. Use this information to figure out first how to help that person be successful.

Next, determine what chain of events lead to that person's placement in your organization. Was the hiring process too speedy? Were there an adequate number of qualified applicants? Was someone inappropriately promoted from within? Was there an interviewing process in place? What kinds of questions were asked in the interview? What was the format of the interview? These are the issues discussed throughout the rest of this book.

Costs – Improperly Placed Employees

Ineffective Element	Effect on Organization	Short-Term	Long-Term			
Turnover costs						
Low productivity						
Low morale						
Frustration of good employees						
Conflicts						
Poor customer service						

Continued . . .

Costs – Improperly Placed Employees

Ineffective Element	Effect on Organization	Short-Term	Long-Term		
Knowledge of job inadequate					
Ability to do job inadequate					
Willingness to do job inadequate					
Inappropriate behavior					
Inefficient use of resources					
Other:					

Now that you know what a bad hire costs you, let's take a look at what a good hire can mean.

What a Good Hire Means to an Organization

Good hires are winners for you, the department, and the organization. They are achievers who figure out how to work smarter to accomplish their role and the goals within the organization. Because they are already peak achievers, they require less time in training, need less supervision, and are already motivated to do their best. In addition to adding to the organization's productivity, they also decrease expenses through reduced turnover costs involved in recruiting and hiring.

Getting the right people in the right jobs will take your organization to the next level of profitability. To help you achieve this goal, the following section will give you some guidelines on how to hire right the first time.

Four Strategies for Hiring Right

1. Develop a Hiring System

This is a step that is surprisingly forgotten by many organizations. Having a hiring system is as important as setting earnings goals or having a departmental budget. Without a plan and a structure in which to execute the plan, your hiring system simply cannot be effective.

When putting your system together, the key component is communication. Do not allow your organization to sabotage itself with turf wars. In some organizations, tensions arise between departments with open positions and Human Resources personnel. The perception is that going through HR is time consuming, and some desirable candidates might be lost if too much time is taken. To speed up the process, some managers circumvent Human Resources and have potential candidates apply directly to them. While the frustration is understandable, it is problematic. If there is a clear hiring system already in place, it is not working due to lack of attention or effective communication.

If you don't have a specific procedure, now is the time to formulate one. Here are some things to keep in mind when creating or streamlining your hiring system:

- Establish clear lines of communication between departments and Human Resources.

- If the process is taking too long, or is too cumbersome, determine the causes and figure out the solutions as interdepartmental teams. It is important to the overall strength of your organization and system that grievances are aired and changes are made to meet the needs of the parties involved.

- Decide who will screen the applications and resumes.

- Select the methods of pre-hire screenings your organization will use. Will there be tests to take? Applications to fill out? Phone interviews?

- Figure out what you would like the candidates to bring to the interview. Additional references? A portfolio of work?

- Establish the type of interview, the number of interviews, and who will be involved.

- Determine who will be involved in the decision to hire.

- Be clear on who will orient and help the new hire during the transition.

- Revisit the process at least once a year to see how effectively the system is working for you, what concerns there might be, and how to adapt and move forward.

Everyone in your hiring system needs to be empowered to do what is best for the organization. Not only do you need to attract qualified candidates, you need to filter out the ill-equipped or uninterested candidates. When fewer unqualified people slip through, the entire process of recruiting and hiring will become tighter and more reliable. Establish your system and motivate and empower the key players to make necessary and timely decisions. Do what it takes to hire the best people for the position—this should be your organization's mantra.

Take a moment to establish what you will do to implement or perfect your hiring system. Brainstorm all possible elements and parties involved.

Hiring System Action Steps

Action Steps to Implement or Change Hiring System	Individuals/ Departments Involved	Completion Date
1.		
2.		
3.		
4.		
5.		

Continued . . .

Hiring System Action Steps

Action Steps to Implement or Change Hiring System	Individuals/ Departments Involved	Completion Date
6.		
7.		
8.		
9.		
10.		

2. Understand the Job You Are Trying to Fill

To hire the best person for the job, you must know what the job requires. It is a good idea to conduct a job analysis of the position you are hiring for. If you *really* want to be ahead, conduct an analysis of every position within your organization. Spending the time on job analyses can save a lot of time and money down the road by providing you with:

- Accurate job descriptions
- Hiring ad material
- Interview questions
- Performance evaluation checklists
- Data for training needs
- Data for organizational planning

You can create your own job analysis, or you can use one of the many tools that are packaged and available today. Depending on the tool or method you use, you can spend 3 hours or 3 weeks on a job analysis. (See Appendix A.)

Determine the needs of this position from as many perspectives as possible—don't be fooled into thinking you know everything about the position unless you have worked it recently. There is great value in keeping current with those who have direct contact with the person in this position. Not only are you gathering information in order to accurately place a new hire, you are also giving a voice to those within your organization who would like to see something change within the position.

Process for Job Analysis.

The job analysis process involves the following steps:

A. **Involve the key players**. These include top performers who already fill that position, managers, supervisors, and Human Resources. Getting feedback from all of these people will help you get an accurate idea of what it takes to be successful in the position.

B. **Establish core areas**. These are the major responsibilities of the position.

C. **Identify task list.** These are the specific tasks associated with each of the core areas.

D. **Gain agreement.** The key players need to agree that the analysis you have determined is accurate, thorough, and representative of the requirements and needs of the position.

For example, let's say you are a financial institution seeking to fill a financial planner position. With your key players in the process, you might break down the main responsibility or core areas like this:

Core 1: Product Knowledge
Core 2: Process Knowledge
Core 3: Sales Knowledge
Core 4: Compliance and Regulatory
Core 5: Interpersonal Skills
Core 6: Administrative

Next, establish the necessary tasks for each one. This is an abbreviated sample to give you an idea.

Core Area	Tasks
Product Knowledge	Understand specific features and benefits of life insurance contracts.
	Understand specific features and benefits of managed investments.
	Understand specific features and benefits of fixed and variable annuities.
	Use Investmentview™ to research investment products.
	Use Foresight™ to research insurance products.

Core Area	Tasks
Process Knowledge	Apply tax strategies
	Suggest appropriate retirement plans/accounts
	Recommend appropriate college savings
	Recommend appropriate form of ownership
	Understand proper use of wills, trusts, estate planning techniques
Sales Knowledge	Identify prospects
	Approach/open with client
	Conduct needs analysis
	Present findings
	Close the sale
Compliance & Regulatory	Know laws and regulations for conducting business
	Submit all sales material to Compliance for approval prior to use
	Maintain records for all client accounts
	Copy all correspondence
	Prepare for audits and reviews

Core Area	Tasks
Interpersonal Skills	Utilize presentation skills
	Communicate ideas effectively
	Utilize listening skills to determine customer needs and wants
	Maintain good working relationships with supervisor and co-workers
	Maintain positive attitude
	Use PowerPoint™ to deliver client seminars
Administrative	Execute timely correspondence
	Complete relevant forms and applications
	Utilize effective time management skills
	Provide necessary documentation to financial product providers
	Resolve service issues for clients

As you are identifying core areas and tasks, also take an inventory of the specific technical skills the position requires. For example, in the above task list, this person would either need to know the Foresight™ software program or would need to be trained in it. These details are helpful when writing job descriptions or job advertisements.

Lastly, gain agreement from all those involved. Use this process as the basis for your employee search and incorporate it into your hiring system.

3. Conduct Structured Interviews

An unstructured interview is where you come to the interview with an idea of what you'd like to find out, but nothing is formalized or systematic. A structured interview is where you have very clearly identified questions, both in content and form, that are asked of all the candidates alike. Recruiting and hiring specialists find that structured interviews are far more valuable and give better information than unstructured interviews do because they rely less on instinct and more on data.

4. Use Behavioral Interviewing

Behavioral interviewing is based on the idea that the best predictor of future work performance is in past performance. This method of interviewing has been found to be extremely effective by hiring managers because it focuses on the candidate's ability to do the job rather than his or her ability to get the job. In the behavioral interview, the interviewer asks the candidate to recall specific examples from his or her past work experience. After the candidate provides an answer, the interviewer asks the candidate to detail the specific steps or actions they took and the corresponding results.

It takes time to develop the necessary skills to ask the appropriate questions and follow up with probing questions. You will practice using behavioral interview questions in the following chapters.

Recently, some organizations have begun to ask their prospective employees to actually perform duties that they would find on the job. Let's say you are looking for someone to manage your call center. Present them with the organizational flow for the department, provide them with specific staffing or sales challenges, and ask them to draw up a solution. Based on the questions they ask, the information they require, and the solution they come up with, you have a good idea of how this person would perform on the job.

If you do not want certain sensitive information about your organization to be so openly shared, consider using a similar problem in every regard: the nature of the problem, the number of people involved, the required materials or information, and the scope of the project should all be like the situations an employee would encounter on the job.

Write Effective Job Descriptions

If you cannot effectively describe the position, you cannot effectively hire for it. Oftentimes, historical assumptions about the background, education, and skills necessary to do a job shape job descriptions. Analyze these carefully. If the current description says the candidate needs to have 10 years of experience, why is that? If there is a clear rationale, then include it. What if a well-qualified candidate with 8½ years of experience wants to apply but doesn't based on the description? What if the same person does apply, but your screening process eliminates him or her based on that one requirement? Review each of the performance requirements you established in the job analysis and ask these questions:

- What does the person need to be able to do?
- What kind of initial evidence would indicate this person can do the job?
- Are these historical assumptions?
- If the candidate does not have the "traditional" education or experience, what other evidence would tell you he or she could perform the duties of this position?

Take a look at the current job description you have on file for the position you need to fill. Is it accurate? Does it match up with the job analysis you performed on that position? Refer back to the job analysis that we created earlier in this chapter to see how well it lends itself to creating a job description.

Job Description:
Financial Planner

This position involves providing financial planning for clients. The employee will need to have current product knowledge of insurance and investment products. Employee needs to be familiar with Insight™ and Investmentview™ research vehicles. This person will be knowledgeable in the various processes and strategies of financial planning in order to apply tax strategies, suggest appropriate retirement plans, recommend appropriate college savings, recommend appropriate form of ownership, and understand the proper use of wills, trusts, and estate planning techniques. The employee will need to execute the sales process, from identifying prospects to closing the sale. The employee will execute all necessary compliance and administrative tasks to prepare for audits and reviews. The employee will demonstrate interpersonal skills to uncover customer needs and maintain a positive attitude. The employee should have a good working knowledge of presentation tools such as Microsoft PowerPoint™ to deliver client seminars. Employee will follow all administrative guidelines to execute timely correspondence, complete forms and applications, provide necessary documentation, and resolve service issues for clients. Employee will utilize effective time management by using Microsoft Outlook™. This employee must have series 7, 63, and 65 designations. The employee needs to have at least 3 years of experience or demonstrate the ability to assimilate the core duties of this position.

You may get as detailed as you like with the job description. The example above included the core areas and many of the skills necessary.

Think for a moment about a position in your organization with which you are very familiar. Using the information provided so far in this chapter, sketch out a comprehensive job description for that position.

Job Title: _____

You can well imagine how having an accurate and current job description on file will help draw qualified candidates. The less time you have to spend screening unqualified or uninformed candidates, the better. This makes your job easier and the overall hiring system more efficient.

Top 5 Ideas from this Chapter

- Hiring a new person can cost up to 30 to 100 percent of the employee's salary.

- A good hire increases productivity, reduces expenses, and carries your organization to a new level in the marketplace.

- A systematic hiring system is essential to effective recruitment and placement.

- Conducting a job analysis and behavioral interview will provide information for hiring and beyond.

- Effective job descriptions make your job a lot easier.

Chapter Two:
Recruiting Strategies

Chapter Objectives

This chapter covers strategies to help you:

- ➢ Create your own recruitment pipeline.
- ➢ Find new ways to attract the best candidates.
- ➢ Explore your recruiting options.
- ➢ Use the Internet to aid your search.
- ➢ Find nontraditional candidates.

Gone are the days when a position would open up in an organization, an ad would be placed, four rounds of interviews would be conducted, and a suitable person would be hired for the position and could, very feasibly, remain in the organization for the next 25 years. Things are changing in the workplace. People are changing jobs at an alarming rate, the rate of unemployment is decidedly low, and our concept of what the workplace and the nature of our work should be changes by the year. Because of this, more pressure than ever is being placed on hiring managers to find and keep qualified and valuable employees in their organizations.

It all begins with recruiting. You can have the best organization, the best jobs, the best of everything, but unless you can attract people to apply for your open positions, your fate is sealed. The workforce is, and will continue to be, increasingly diverse. Hiring managers and departments need to think beyond the traditional approach to recruiting—the talent *is* out there. This chapter deals with new ideas to incorporate into your recruiting plan. Take these ideas and incorporate them to best suit you, but go beyond the ideas offered if other ones come to you. The key to the new recruiting style is to get creative. Determine where in the market a number of likely candidates will be, then find a way to access them. You might also want to contact professional organizations in your area or related fields to stay current with any new methods being used.

Remember that in all of your recruiting efforts, weeding out the wrong or uninterested candidates is just as important as attracting good candidates. Uninterested candidates are the biggest risk for losing money. They could be great for the position, but if they are not at all motivated to move, you are wasting your efforts. The uninterested candidate is like the neighbor attending an open house on your recently listed home; they just want to see the inside with no intention of buying the house. These candidates might want to find out more about you, but do not intend to "buy."

Reflect for a moment on the number of new hires you have had during the past year. How did they find out about you? Were they recruited by word of mouth? Classified advertising? What? List out all of the recruitment strategies and methods that your organization currently uses, and how many people were placed due to that method.

Analyze Recruitment Methods

Recruitment Method	# New Hires Produced
1.	
2.	
3.	
4.	
5.	
6.	
7.	
8.	
9.	
10.	

When it comes to filling a position, the most effective hiring system will be meaningless unless you can get qualified applicants. The ideas presented in this chapter are for you to take and tailor to fit your specific needs. You may have other sources not listed here—that's good! The more creative, resourceful, and comprehensive your networking system, the better your chances of finding the perfect fit will be.

Create a Pipeline

You should work as hard to create a pipeline of candidates as you do to create a pipeline of business. It is not enough to search for the people who are actively looking for jobs; you need to consider those who might not be actively looking as well. A recent survey cited in the *New York Times* found that half of the managers responding over the age of 35 talk to headhunters at least quarterly. There are always some people who could be cultivated and interested in the positions you have to offer. Capitalize on this. Establish solid relationships with people wherever you go; every person you meet could be a future employee.

How many people do you talk to about your organization and the potential within it when you are not specifically looking to fill a position?

Try to position yourself in the marketplace as a business where people are waiting in line for interviews and are pleased with the organization and their jobs after they've been hired. What you yourself put out there can go great lengths in achieving this goal.

Make Your Organization Attractive to Potential Candidates

The workplace is changing rapidly. On-site fitness centers, on-site daycare centers, lactation rooms, and recreation centers are just a few of the changes we've seen in the past few years. Another big change is flexibility in job structure. Many employers are finding that employees are looking for a better balance between work and home responsibilities. With the remarkable capabilities of modern technology, physical space is becoming less important, and employers are finding they can capitalize on this.

Evaluate the positions you have and ask yourself if there is room for flexible, nontraditional work options. For example, consider a job-sharing program that splits the work week in half for two employees. You can have each person work 4½ hours each day, or perhaps split the week with each person working 2½ days. There are also job shares where one person works 2 days one week and 3 the next, with the other person taking the alternate days. Consider, too, if a compressed workweek would work for your organization. This typically is a 4-day week, 10 hours per day. Programs such as these are attractive to many people who need additional time to balance work with home and are also good morale boosters. If you are thinking of experimenting with these, make sure it is feasible for your organization and the work required of the position. Try it in one department or area to see how effective it would be.

Telecommuting from home is also on the rise with many organizations. If the job can be performed at home with a computer, fax, and e-mail, consider this nontraditional approach to employee environment. The flexibility to the employee is tremendous. For example, if the employee does his or her best work at night, then you are capitalizing on productivity and creativity that might otherwise be lost. This is also a viable way to save on space. Many organizations are decreasing their expenses by scaling down the physical size of their operations and saving on real estate costs. This could be a very affordable way to do business as well.

These programs are very attractive to many job seekers, but there are some business considerations as well. If the nature of the work does not allow these types of arrangements, then think about what flexibility you can offer, if any. Be sure to incorporate these employees as members of the team, even though they are not there as much. Be creative and purposeful in doing this so that employees do not feel disenfranchised. Find ways to show your appreciation, have regular meetings, and keep the lines of communication wide open.

Where to Look?

Within Your Organization

Do what you can to prevent employees from leaving in the first place. We've already seen how costly one instance of employee turnover can be. Communicate regularly with your employees and have an open-door policy. If they are discontent in their position, encourage them to come to you before seeking out other opportunities. They will appreciate being heard and seeing the possibilities for them-selves with the organization. You may have a chance to challenge that employee in ways you did not know they wanted. Open communication will go a long way in keeping your employees to begin with.

When you do have a position to fill however, a logical first step is to post the position within your organization. You may have an untapped gold mine of potential right under your nose. Let employees know exactly what the position entails and the qualities you are looking for in the candidates. An added benefit here is that some of the unknown variables that exist when considering a candidate can be avoided. For instance, you have ready access to the employee's performance within his or her department. Ask for an opinion regarding the employee's strengths, their likes and dislikes in their current position, and what their specific performance challenges might be, if any. Keep in mind, however, that the manager's assessment should only help you decide if the employee should get an interview. Many personal biases, while they shouldn't enter in, sometimes do.

You might want to consider administering competency assessments periodically to your existing employees in order to determine what resources you already have in your labor pool should an opening become available. This is another way you can use the job analysis for each position. Review the employee's job analysis, compare with the manager's assessment of performance in each area, and focus on the transferable skills.

Another thing to keep in mind is to follow the same hiring system and guidelines you've established. Many times, hiring managers will skip over key elements when considering internal candidates. Do not make assumptions about the employee's performance or potential. Follow the hiring process. Remain as objective here as you would be with any other candidate. It is always a good idea to remain consistent both in criteria and process regardless of who the candidate is, or where he or she comes from. This consistency may help avoid any liability issues when disgruntled candidates are not offered a position.

Traditional Advertising

There are two kinds of advertising here: organization advertising and specific position advertising. It is important to your overall recruiting scheme that your organization's name is out in the community. Raise the level of awareness of what your organization specializes in, what kind of an environment it is, and any other positive selling points that you would like people to know when they think of your organization. You can accomplish a great deal through newspaper ads about your organization, billboards, and radio and local television ads. Always be on the lookout for new and creative ways to get your name out into the community.

When you have specific positions to fill, the time and resources you have put into your organization advertising can be a definite plus. Obviously, when people have positive feelings and thoughts about your organization you are more likely to attract qualified individuals. When placing specific ads, local newspapers, trade journals, and other professional publications are excellent options.

The better the ad, the better the applicant. Highlight the essential qualities needed to perform the job, and list required skills and education. You should already have the job description written—from this you can create your ad.

Pay attention to the size of your ad; many ads are too big and unnecessarily costly. In order for this to be an effective method of recruiting, the return on investment needs to make sense. Keep it succinct but powerful; avoid lengthy descriptions of the organization and unnecessary use of adjectives and adverbs. Also, avoid being overly creative in the expression. Many times the wording of ads can be inspiring, but without giving the applicant more substance, you may miss out on many potential employees. Be clear on job title, salary range, requirements and performance objectives, and contact information. Anything else is just costing you money. You might even consider limiting your ad to the qualifications necessary then require applicants to tailor their resumes to show how they fulfill each requirement.

Here are some samples of ineffective newspaper advertisements.

Creative? Call (phone number).

This ad is only helpful if you want 10 times as many applicants as you need, and most of them will be unqualified. There is not enough specific information for this to be an effective part of your recruiting strategy.

Frustrated? Just want your chance? Or need a change? Sharp, friendly people wanted. Will train. Top $$. Call (phone number).

This ad gives a little more information, but, again, it will attract way too many unqualified candidates. This organization will also have to take time to address the curious—those individuals who are not really interested, but wanted to know more about it. This costs valuable time and resources for no clear gain.

State University—Department of Residence, one of the largest student housing operations in the country, is seeking candidates for the position for Accountant III. State University is one of the nation's leading universities and enrolls 25,000 students, with more than 8,000 living in the residence halls. In addition, the Department of Residence employs a staff of nearly 1,000 student and full-time employees. Learn more about us at (web address).

This position will provide daily supervision of the departmental accounting and payroll process, including maintenance of an electronic time-keeping system. Create meaningful ad hoc reports and analyses involving financial and other business information. Ensure the integrity of financial information and the security of resources. Collaborate with the Assistant Director—Business Operations to formulate a comprehensive budget and price/cost model for a complex organization. Recommend, develop, and implement appropriate finance tools and electronic systems.

Required qualifications include: Bachelor's degree in accounting or related field plus 2 years experience working with electronic systems in a financial office setting, experience using spreadsheet and database software, and supervisory experience. Preferred qualifications include experience with fund accounting, specifically in a higher education environment, and experience with Microsoft suite of tools.

The normal hiring range is $31,328 – $38,178, commensurate with experience. The University also offers a very attractive benefits package. To guarantee consideration, applications must be received no later than February 15, 2001. Send cover letter and resume along with name, address, and phone number of three references to Chair, Search Committee, (address).

The final ad gives an abundance of useful information. However, it is not a good use of advertising dollars because it is way too long. In order for classified advertising to make sense, the costs must not outweigh the gains. In this case, a great deal of expense was incurred from this one ad, and that is for only one run. Another discrepancy within the ad is that they are looking for someone with 2 years of experience, to include supervisory experience. This might not be a realistic expectation, and they should revisit the outcomes of the position.

There are some pieces of information that would be additionally helpful to your potential candidates. For example, if your organization has a drug screening policy, list this in the requirements section of the ad. That way, there are no surprises for the applicant. It's also a good idea to mention that you are an Equal Opportunity Employer at the bottom of your ad if this is your organization's policy. Check with your organization's legal or compliance department for additional guidelines that may apply specifically to your organization or your industry.

Now, take a look at an effective ad. Again, the information for this ad was pulled from the job description that came from the job analysis completed earlier.

Financial Planner

This position involves providing financial planning for clients. The candidate must possess current knowledge of insurance and investment products, and be knowledgeable in the various processes and strategies of financial planning. The candidate will need to demonstrate proven sales success. Candidate will be able to complete compliance and administrative tasks, and will demonstrate excellent interpersonal skills.

Qualified candidates must have a good working knowledge of Insight™, Investmentview™, and Microsoft PowerPoint™.

Series 7, 63, and 65 licenses are required. Three years of experience or proven ability to assimilate the core responsibilities is required. Salary range is $55,000 – $65,000. Interested candidates should contact Mrs. Helen Robinson at (321) 555-5432. EEO employer.

Now, think of a position that could open up within the next year. Using the above guidelines, practice writing your own effective and economical job advertisement.

One last note on newspaper ads: call your newspaper to find out when most of the employment ads run and if there are any package deals on advertising. Some papers include a run in Monday's paper for free with an ad placed in the Sunday paper.

Employee Incentive Programs

Your employees are a valuable resource when recruiting; good employees generally give good referrals. More and more organizations are offering their employees incentives when they are instrumental in recruiting someone to the organization. Many organizations pay hundreds and even thousands of dollars for a successful referral. The "finder's fee" is typically not paid to the employee until the new hire has been on the job for a certain amount of time, but these arrangements have proven to be very effective for finding and hiring excellent candidates.

Vendors and Customers

These groups are often overlooked. The people with whom you do business know your organization and how you conduct business, and are therefore an excellent touch point when you are trying to fill a position. They are also connected with other professionals in many geographic areas as well as specialty areas and may have an extensive list of contacts. You never know where a good lead may come from, so look everywhere.

Minority Groups/Organizations

Contact the groups in your area that specialize in the promotion and advocacy of minority groups. You will find that if your organization does not have employees from a variety of backgrounds, you could be missing out on a great share of the market. By becoming more diverse, you will also attract more qualified candidates from all backgrounds who want to work and create and in a stimulating environment.

Employment Agencies

These organizations are primarily candidate geared. They spend a great deal of time educating potential candidates on how to write a resume, how to prepare for an interview, and how to conduct themselves in an interview—basically, how to get hired. When organizations that list with that particular agency need candidates, the employment agent scans through the databases to find individuals with the required skill set. Most states have state-run employment agencies, but check to see what other specialty employment agencies are in your area.

Recruiting/Staffing Firms

Just as the employment agencies focus more on the candidates, these firms focus their attention on the organizations. They often specialize in a specific industry (e.g., financial, technology), so find out which firms would be of greatest benefit to you. Your organization provides them with the specifications for the job, and they spend time looking for you. They may draw upon the pool of candidates they already have, may advertise, or otherwise find referrals to help you find a good hire. This is a very active kind of recruiting. When organizations call with a need, some recruiters will begin to call people in similar positions with other organizations. When they have found the technical and performance skill sets you require, the recruiter evaluates the qualities and qualifications of the candidates, and passes on the best to you. The unique thing about these firms is that many of the people they will place in new positions already have jobs and are happy with them. These employees are in an excellent position; they don't need to have a job to pay the bills, or want to get away from a poor organization or manager; they are considering your position because they want to.

Recruiting firms typically charge a fee based on a percentage of the employee's salary, which is paid by the organization. Since you are not at all obligated unless you hire someone through them, this is a very effective vehicle if you do not have a lot of time to spend on the search. If you decide to use a recruiting firm, there are several points to be aware of in order to maximize your relationship.

- **Evaluate their track record.** Establish how long the firm has been doing business, who their customers are, and which industries they specialize in. Obtain professional references from them, and follow up with these carefully. Your time, money, and organization reputation are all at stake if you injudiciously use an ill-qualified firm.

- **Meet face to face with the recruiter.** If the recruiter won't come to your job site, this is a big red flag. Good recruiters know that the needs assessment they perform will help them to do a better job for you. In order to give you good candidates, they first need to know what your need is, and what it is like to work at your organization.

- **Focus.** Recruiting firms may not give you their best efforts if you are using several at once. If you are using several recruiters at once, the chances of one recruiter's candidates getting placed in your positions drastically decreases. If you have an open position and five or six recruiters looking for you, each spending the time to find, evaluate, and recommend their top three candidates for your consideration, then you have to spend time evaluating the 15 to 18 resumes that are submitted. The process becomes redundant and time consuming, good candidates might get turned away simply because there are too many to review, and you, the recruiter, and the candidates suffer. In such futile situations good recruiters might refuse to do business with you in the future and might steer excellent candidates away from you. Look for good recruiters who truly want to establish a long-term relationship with you and act on good faith with the agreement. Everyone will profit from this kind of arrangement.

Temporary Job Placement Firms

Many temporary agencies are also full-time staffing firms. If you need to fill a position for a short amount of time, have an immediate need for help while you search for and recruit a new person, or just want to try to fill a position by using a temp, temporary job placement services could be very helpful to you. If you find a temp whom you believe will suit the needs of your organization, then you can fill your position using a temp-to-hire program.

Trade Shows/Conventions

These events are a good source of information about what's happening in your industry, introduce new products or services, and can also be a valuable networking venue. Establishing relationships with other experts helps feed your pipeline with leads when you have a position that needs to be filled. Keep track of the business cards that are given to you. While you don't want to be too blatant with a job offer at one of these events, giving a promotional product from your organization, or at the very least your business card, could be effective in drawing the attention of a possible candidate. You never know who might be looking for a change and why, so always be on the lookout for a possible recruiting opportunity. These events also keep you fresh and in touch with hot topics and trends; being aware of these and incorporating them into your organization may be a selling point with potential employees.

Competition

It is always a good idea to know your competition. This holds true with recruiting as well. By keeping up with trade journals, attending trade shows and seminars, and listening to customers and vendors, you can identify people from other organizations. Send word out through the industry grapevine on which positions you are hiring for. Again, you never know who might be looking for a new challenge.

Job Fairs

If you have a lot of positions to fill, setting up a display during a job fair could be an economical option for you. Job fairs bring together many organizations and hundreds of possible candidates. For the price of a booth fee, you can promote your organization in a general sense for future candidates and can also hunt for people to fill your specific positions.

Other Networking

As a hiring manager, you should always be on the prowl for new talent to join your team. Being a member of charitable events, civic organizations, or other groups such as breakfast clubs is another way for you to meet and talk to people. Establishing relationships with a number of people from all different fields can be very beneficial when it comes time to hire someone new. Whether they know someone or might be interested in the position themselves, the people you meet are valuable resources for you. Talk to the people you know, and meet new people whenever you can—you'll be surprised by the opportunities that present themselves.

Consultants

If your organization uses consultants for certain areas within your business, ask if they know of anyone who might be interested in the position. Consultants come in contact with many people and businesses in a variety of industries and just may have a few leads for you.

Other People You Know

Within your daily routine you come in contact with many people. Your accountant, banker, doctor, dentist, mechanic, old college professor, local restaurant owner, and others are all valuable assets when it comes to recruiting. Talk to the people you know and have daily contact with in your personal or professional life. For every one of those people, another circle of contacts is possible.

Student Summer Jobs

Hiring high school or college students during the summer is a good way to introduce them to your business and also to see if they would be good hires for full-time employment in the future. As with internships, it is important that some time be given to structuring the program so that the student has a positive experience with your organization. Providing them with too much or too little work, or work that is overly redundant could turn them off to your organization and your industry in general. Make sure the program reflects the true nature of the organization and fosters good relationships with those it sponsors.

Internships

In an increasingly tight labor market, looking to nontraditional recruiting methods will become a necessity to fill jobs in the upcoming months and years. By establishing an internship program within your organization, you are strengthening your organization in many ways. These programs enable you to get people into your organization that might otherwise not have been there or even have thought about your industry as a career choice. You can greatly raise the level of awareness about your industry, the organization, and specific positions within the organization that the student might be interested in. High schools, colleges, and universities will view the program favorably because it forges a bridge between school and work. It also will help you to establish relationships with these institutions that could be very valuable to you in the long run. Talking to teachers, guidance counselors, career centers, and professors provides you with another source of leads for potential candidates. This is an option that is not used as much as it should be. With a little planning and communication with local learning institutions, you can go a long way in growing your own talent.

If you implement an internship program, give plenty of time to the planning of the program. If the position is meaningless and serves no purpose other than shadowing someone around, or gives the person too much or too little to do, those who proceed through the program will form a negative impression of your organization. Find ways to cycle the intern through various departments. Let them experience the variety of positions and experiences they can have in your organization. Encourage them to ask questions, and above all make sure the relationship between the intern and his or her mentor is a positive one. Word spreads quickly on campuses as to which organization is beneficial to work for and which is not.

Niche/Contract Employees

Many organizations are hiring niche/contract employees who specialize in a certain area to work on a particular project. These employees can prove to be very valuable. Hiring them alleviates the problem of hiring a full-time person for a project and then having extra staff after the project is over. For example, if your training department is facing an extensive restructuring of program and products, you can contract someone to come in during the timeline of the project. You may have to pay them a little more than you are paying your traditional employees, but you will save in recruiting and training costs, benefit costs, and the expense of having a redundant staff after the need is gone. Find out who specializes in the areas in which you might have a need, and get referrals from them for previous work they have done for other organizations. You might be surprised at how effective and economical this can be.

Using the Internet in Recruiting Efforts

In order to position your organization and attract top performers, establishing a presence on the World Wide Web is essential in today's market. For many people, this is the first place to turn to when considering a change in jobs. Using the Internet to recruit is very economical, and with an experienced web designer who can update your site frequently, it is a stress-free way for you to reach a lot of potential candidates.

In addition to listing your openings on your web site, you can also contact a number of employment search engines. There are employment sites popping up daily. The top 10 sites for employment as of February 2001 are:

- Monster.com
- Welcome to jobs.com
- Galaxy: Employment
- America's Job Bank
- CareerPath.com
- The World Wide Web Employment Office.com
- HotJobs.com
- NationJob.com
- Virtual Employment Center
- Cweb.com (Career Web)

Due to the nature of the Internet, the sites listed may experience name changes. If the sites listed here do not appear in your search, type in key words such as "Employment" or "Careers" to find what you are looking for.

One rule of thumb when listing on job boards is to avoid posting your positions on unpaid sites. It is better when the listing organization is as motivated as you are to continue a mutual relationship. Some sites cost $5,000 to list for a year, others up to $50,000. This does not mean the more you pay the more you get, but it does demonstrate the variety of packages available to you.

In addition to posting nationally, there are many sites devoted to individual state's recruiting efforts, military and civilian. There are also local online job boards springing up all over.

Most sites are organized in the same way. When you log in, you can view how many organizations are currently listing vacancies and how many job seekers have shown interest. Home pages are usually broken down into information specifically for job seekers and another for recruiters. In the recruiting section, you can detail the type of position, what the salary range is, full-time or part-time, and so on. There is another section where you describe the organization and contact information.

This type of service is very inexpensive. In many places, you can post an ad up to 100 words for 30 days for around $100—compare that to other advertising costs and you can quickly see the value of these types of job boards. Investigate the options in your immediate vicinity to see what is available to you.

There are also sites that list the employment sections of hundreds of daily newspapers across the country. Ask your local paper if they too post their listings with an employment search engine.

At www.jobsearchengines.com, you will find a directory of job search engines that are updated every week. There are hundreds of search vehicles on this one site alone, all listed alphabetically and covering dozens of industries and career areas. Contact the sites that appeal to you and find out the terms of listing with their service. Also, find out how often they update their site and how many direct hits they typically receive in a week's time.

One Internet job board, NationJob, has been rated #1 in overall customer satisfaction among Internet job boards according to the Electronic Recruiting News 2000 survey of 3,000 corporate HR professionals and recruiters. NationJob has put together a few tools to aid its clients' hiring process. The ROI Calculator helps you calculate your return on investment when making a decision about using job boards. The 8-Point Checklist helps you post the most effective job listing as possible. Both instruments are on the following pages. This is just a sample of the tools and job aids available to you on the web.

Recruiting Strategies

(Sample) ROI Calculator

NationJob Network
www.nationjob.com

To help you calculate your return on investment from the NationJob service, we've put together the following calculation based on information you've given us about your results. This tool is intended to help you and your management make decisions about NationJob and other recruitment methods.

Your Web Recruiting Specialist _____

Service Dates _____

1. Value

Position title: Customer Service Rep.
Resumes Received __12__   Resumes Qualified __3__
Approximate annual compensation: $ __20,000__
Cost per hire *(at 16% of annual salary)*: $ __3,200__
Likelihood of one placement: (x __50__ %)
Value of service *(cost per hire x likelihood of placement)*: $ __1,600__

Position title: Engineer
Resumes Received __9__   Resumes Qualified __2__
Approximate annual compensation: $ __60,000__
Cost per hire *(at 16% of annual salary)*: $ __9,600__
Likelihood of one placement: (x __30__ %)
Value of service *(cost per hire x likelihood of placement)*: $ __2,880__

Position title: _____
Resumes Received _____   Resumes Qualified _____
Approximate annual compensation: $ _____
Cost per hire *(at 16% of annual salary)*: $ _____
Likelihood of one placement: (x _____ %)
Value of service *(cost per hire x likelihood of placement)*: $ _____

Position title: _____
Resumes Received _____   Resumes Qualified _____
Approximate annual compensation: $ _____
Cost per hire *(at 16% of annual salary)*: $ _____
Likelihood of one placement: (x _____ %)
Value of service *(cost per hire x likelihood of placement)*: $ _____

2. Cost

1. Hours spent listing, updating jobs (after initial set-up) = __1/4__ (x $40/hour) = $ __10__
2. Hours spent reviewing resumes = __3__ hours (x $40/hour) = $ __120__
3. Hours spent on interview process = __4__ hours (x $60/hour) = $ __240__
   416
4. Cost of listing (1/12th of NationJob annual fee) =
   (NationJob Annual Fee __$5,000__)   **Total Cost = $** __786__

3. Value of Service $ 4,800

Total Cost $ __786__
Total Net Value $ __4,014__
(value-cost)
ROI __610__ %
(value-cost)

52

NationJob 8-Point Listing Checklist

Company _____ Name _____

Your Web Recruiting Specialist _____ Phone _____

Your Job Listings are located at _____ Fax _____

Like any recruitment tool, the kind of results you get from NationJob depend on how you use it. **The key to success is to think like a job seeker,** and, based on what job seekers want to see, use your listings to attract qualified applicants and discourage unqualified people.

I've reviewed eight aspects of the listings you've posted. A rating of 1 or 2 indicates a real problem in the specific area, while a rating of 5 is excellent. Numbers in between indicate degrees of room for improvement. I've written in or circled some comments that apply, but as always, feel free to call me directly and I'll be glad to help you in any way that I can.

1. Job Titles   1   2   3   4   5   Think of the job title as the "gatekeeper" to the job listing: if the job seeker isn't interested in reading more after viewing the title, you've lost that potential applicant. **Job titles must be descriptive** (avoid internal company titles and project names if they don't describe the job) and **specific** ("Electrical Engineer" is better than "Engineer;" "Electrical Engineer/Power Supplies" is better still).

2. Salaries   1   2   3   4   5   If you don't think **salary is the most important thing** to job seekers, ask yourself this: would you consider moving to a new job that paid ½ of what you're making now? More and more job seekers refuse to apply for positions that don't list an explicit salary or at least a salary range. Why should they waste their time—and yours—on an application and interview process when you're $20,000 apart on salary? Be specific and explicit and your results will improve greatly.

3. Qualifications clearly detailed? 1 2 3 4 5 The goal of the qualifications section is to discourage unqualified people from responding, but to **encourage everyone who meets your minimum standards to apply.** You must be clear in your own mind who you want resumes from and who you don't, and then express that in your listings. Can a job seeker tell what your minimum requirements are vs. what you prefer the ideal candidate to have? For example, is a degree an absolute requirement or will equivalent experience do?

4. Duties clearly detailed? 1 2 3 4 5 Job seekers read the description of the duties to **answer the questions: "Do I want to do this job?"** and **"Would I be good at this job?"** Titles can only tell a job seeker so much—two similarly-titled positions may encompass very different daily activities. Use complete descriptions (including who the position reports to) and avoid internal company jargon. This will increase qualified response and discourage unqualified applicants. Why wait for the interview to explain the job when you can do it online?

5. Company background/ profile? 1 2 3 4 5 Does your information answer the basic questions about your company? **Can the job seeker tell what your company does,** what industry you're in, if you're a large or a small company, established or a start-up, and what your work environment/philosophy is? Some of this information—particularly industry—should be in the job description; all of it should be in your company profile. Most companies have this type of descriptive information somewhere: if you can just send it to us in any form, we can do the work to put it online for you.

6. Company benefits/ personality   1   2   3   4   5   **What sets your company apart?** Casual work environment? Are you #1 in your industry in a certain category? Friday happy hours? Great internal advancement/ training opportunities? There are things about your company that the right applicant will like: sell them!

7. How to apply   1   2   3   4   5   If ten jobs matched your basic preferences, and you could apply to nine of them by e-mailing a resume and the tenth required filling out a long application form, **which one would you skip applying for?** On the other hand, if you knew a company was specifi- cally interested in you for a position you wanted, taking 10 – 15 minutes to fill out a form would be seen as a good investment. The best way to use online applications is to first request resumes via e-mail, review them, then send e-mails back to the applicants you're interested in with a link to the form online.

8. Tracking   1   2   3   4   5   Giving job seekers multiple ways to apply (fax, mail, multiple e-mail addresses, phone, a link through your web site, walk-in, etc.) can generate more results. However, it also makes these results much more difficult to track. **The more ways you open up for applicants to apply, the harder it is to attribute a source.** *Note:* low ratings in this category don't necessarily mean that anything needs to be changed; they're more a warning about how hard it will be to measure results from NationJob.

Other Comments:

NationJob: Rated #1 in Overall Customer Satisfaction among Internet job boards. *Source: Electronic Recruiting News 2000 survey of 3,000 corporate HR professionals and recruiters.*

E-mail

Another tool your computer affords you is the use of e-mail. For many of us, e-mail is as essential as having a cup of coffee in the morning. It is a fast and effective means of communication and is a powerful recruiting tool. When you are searching for a new employee, send the message out to your mail list. Be sure to include all return correspondence in your message, and then wait to see who follows up with you.

Nontraditional Candidates

Some suggestions have already been given in this chapter to attract as many people as you can from a number of sources. In the coming years there will be fewer people to fill all of the baby boomers' jobs, and in an already tight labor market, this could be a difficult problem for many organizations. It bears repeating that nontraditional candidates could be a way to solve the shortage.

Here are some tips:

- Seek out and encourage women, minorities, older workers, younger workers, and individuals with special needs to join your organization.

- Establish relationships with local schools, colleges, universities, or other post-secondary institutions.

- Find ways to offer flexibility and restructure the positions that are conducive to the job. Consider job share opportunities or telecommuting.

- Focus on candidate competence rather than extensive past experience.

- Develop internship programs and summer work programs.

As a result of this chapter, what are some ideas you would like to implement in your recruiting process? When will the elements be in place?

Recruiting Action Plan

Recruitment Method	Timeline
1.	
2.	
3.	
4.	
5.	
6.	
7.	
8.	
9.	
10.	

Top 5 Ideas from this Chapter

- Creativity is the key to effective recruiting in today's market.

- Talk to anyone you come in contact with, even when you are not actively seeking to fill a position. It is important to build these relationships before the need arises.

- Evaluate your recruiting ads to eliminate skills and background requirements that are based on historical assumptions. Keep only what is current and accurate to performing the duties of the position.

- The Internet is a powerful recruiting tool.

- Nontraditional candidates could go a long way in solving your recruiting and hiring crises.

Chapter Three:
Prepare for Your Interview

Chapter Objectives

This chapter covers strategies to help you:

- ➢ Design questions for the interview.
- ➢ Understand types of questions to ask.
- ➢ Utilize strategies to get the most out of the candidate.
- ➢ Determine the interview medium.
- ➢ Prepare your interview location.
- ➢ Consider legal issues.

As your hiring system provides you with qualified candidates, it is time to focus on preparing for the interviews that will begin soon. You cannot prepare too much for interviews—knowing more ahead of time will help you while you are face to face with the candidates.

Design Questions for the Interview

Now that you have gathered extensive information about the needs and requirements of the position, you need to focus on the questions you will ask during the interview.

Many hiring managers believe they have a good grasp of what they want to ask in the interview, but they don't take time to reflect, plan, and write down the actual questions as they pertain to the needs of the position. Having a plan increases your ability to focus on the job and the person's ability to do the job; without a plan, you are subject to forgetting something that is important, spending too much time on one area, or, worse yet, asking questions that are personal in nature and not related to the job. (These kinds of questions are also illegal and will be dealt with in more detail later in the chapter.) Remaining consistent will also shield you from any liability that may arise due to a disgruntled candidate who feels the process was unfair or biased.

When you are designing your questions, focus only on the candidate's:

- Skills

- Experience

- Ability to apply past skills and experience to the job

- Preference for the kind of work required

- Level of motivation

- Aptitude (in absence of an aptitude test)

Questions that do not relate to the above list should not be asked because they have no direct bearing on the person's ability to fulfill the needs of the job.

Your hiring team should determine the categories that the questions are based on. The core areas and related tasks are only one part.

Now that you have categories for your questions, start formulating behavioral-based questions. Rely on the information you established during the job analysis for the core area questions.

Criteria	Details to Support
Skills and Experience	
Core Area	
Core Area	
Core Area	
Core Area	

Continued . . .

Motivation			
Eagerness for more responsibility			
Willingness to work			
Commitment to lifelong learning			

Continued . . .

Ability to Add Value/Apply Experience			
Ability to create opportunity			
Quality of work			
Ability to transfer skills and knowledge			

Continued . . .

Aptitude
Aptitude for critical thinking/problem solving

Sample—Create Behavioral Interview Questions

You can take any category or task and make them into behavioral-based interview questions. The example shows how easily you can adapt the skills/categories list into effective interview questions.

- Provide an example of a time …

- Describe an instance where you …

- Tell me about a time when you demonstrated …

Finding answers to these questions will give you excellent information about how the candidate would perform in this position if hired. Again, remember that in behavioral interviewing past performance is the best indicator of future performance, and all of your questioning efforts should revolve around that one idea.

Criteria	Details to Support
Skills and Experience	
Core Area: Process Knowledge • Apply tax strategies	• Describe an instance when you were required to apply tax strategies to client investments.
Core Area: Interpersonal • Effective presentation skills • Positive attitude	• Provide an example of a time when you used effective presentation skills. • Tell me about a time when you demonstrated a positive attitude in a difficult situation.

Continued . . .

Motivation	
Eagerness for more responsibility	• Detail a time when you showed eagerness and readiness to take on more responsibility.
Willingness to work	• Describe an example of how you show a willingness to work.
Commitment to lifelong learning	• Provide an example of a time where you demonstrated a commitment to lifelong learning.

Continued . .

Ability to Add Value/Apply Experience	
Ability to create opportunity	• Tell me about a time when you created an opportunity within your department.
Quality of work	• Provide an example of a time when you were proud of your quality of work.
Ability to transfer skills and knowledge	• Give examples of how you have transferred the knowledge from one position to another.

Continued . .

Aptitude	
Aptitude for critical thinking/ problem solving	• Provide an example of an instance where you used critical problem solving skills.

Types of Questions

While the questions should be behavior based, there are different types of questions to help you get the most out of the interview. Different questions have different effects and purposes. Using the right question at the right time will help you set the environment you need to promote discussion and will help you discover important information about the candidate.

1. **Rapport-building questions.** These are the questions or comments at the beginning of the interview that enable you to put the candidate at ease and to begin the conversation. While the answers to your questions can be very informative, the main purpose of these questions is to create a comfortable environment in which the candidate feels he or she can open up and talk to you. You can learn a great deal about someone by listening to the words they choose and their enthusiasm about certain topics. Encourage them to talk—establishing this positive climate early will cause the candidate to feel comfortable talking with you and giving you the specific information you need to make a good hiring decision.

    Examples of rapport-building questions are:

    *   Good morning, Evan. I've been looking forward to meeting you and discussing the

details of this position. I notice from your application that you received an award at IBM for streamlining a key process. Tell me the nature of the award and how improving this process affected the department and the organization.

- Hello, Andrea, I'm Jay. I appreciate your interest in this position. In reviewing your resume, I notice that you moved here a few years ago from the Midwest. In your opinion, what are the most significant differences between these two areas of the country?

- Welcome, Susan. I hope the office manager was helpful to you when you arrived—we like to make everyone welcome and comfortable here. In reviewing your resume, I notice in the "Hobbies" section you listed that you are an avid reader. What kinds of books or periodicals do you prefer to read?

2. **Open-ended questions that focus on past behaviors.** These are questions that require more than "yes" or "no" answers and that focus on the specifics of the candidate's past performance. Open-ended questions cannot be answered using just a few words, and therefore the candidate is encouraged to develop his or her answers to give you the valuable information you need.

Refer again to the areas of questioning you should focus on. Your job, based on your understanding of the position for which you are hiring, is to find out if the person can do the job, likes the work, can transfer skills to this position, is motivated, and has aptitude for the work. Develop your questions around these topics to get the candidate to talk about how he or she handled a difficult situation, solved a particular problem, created a new product, etc. Here are some examples of open-ended questions:

- To what extent are you successful in your current position?

- To what extent did your previous position challenge you?

- This job involves analyzing the market for potential opportunities. Tell me about an instance when you identified a niche for your organization and the steps you took to favorably position your organization.

- This position requires a team-based approach to business. Think of a time when you had to bring a team together to accomplish a goal and what the end result was.

- Please think of a situation in which you had to intervene with conflict management strategies. How did you approach the problem and motivate the participants toward a solution?

3. **Probing/Follow-up questions**. These questions help you gather the specifics that relate to the necessary skills. There are several reasons why an applicant might be having difficulty answering the questions to your satisfaction. Sometimes, candidates are just simply nervous and need prompting on the specifics that would be appropriate. You may have a poorly worded question and the applicant is confused, or perhaps they didn't hear the whole question. If they partially answer your question, they may be having trouble gathering their thoughts, forgot one half of the question, or perhaps they are being evasive to hide something. Whatever the reason, probing questions will help you to help them give you the information you need. If they still cannot, then they are either ill suited for the job or are purposefully not detailing a negative incident. This is informative as well. Here are some examples of probing questions:

- You mentioned earlier that you have excellent interpersonal skills. To what do you attribute this ability?

- What about research skills? Do you have as much confidence in your ability here as you do with product development, or is this something you could improve a little?

- You referenced the fact that you were working while pursuing a degree. How many hours a week did you work at your job, and how many credit hours did you take each semester?

- You answered all of my previous questions except for why you left your previous position. Tell me the situation, and how you feel about it now.

Think about an interview you will be conducting in the near future. Write out sample questions for rapport-building, open-ended questions for behavioral examples, and probing questions that will help you find the best candidate.

Kinds of Questions

Rapport-building
1.
2.
3.

Open-ended questions for past performance
1.
2.
3.
4.
5.

Probing/Follow-up questions
1.
2.
3.
4.
5.

Strategies to Get the Most Out of the Candidate

Interviews are very stressful situations for most candidates. Therefore, approaching the interview as a conversation rather than an inquisition will help many candidates open up. Here are a few tips in addition to the strategies already mentioned above:

- **Ask non-question questions**. This is a very effective tool to use because there is a psychological difference between asking a question such as

  "Why should we hire you?"

  versus

  "You appear to be qualified for this position. Take a moment to detail what you believe you can bring to our organization, and how we will benefit."

- **Use soft language.** By softening your questions, you are more likely to get better clues about the person and his or her abilities. Soft language feels less threatening to candidates, and they are better able and willing to give you the desired information. Qualifying words and phrases can go a long way. Here are some examples:

  - ❖ Perhaps
  - ❖ Might

- ❖ Somewhat
- ❖ A bit
- ❖ Sometimes
- ❖ To what extent
- ❖ To some extent
- ❖ Is it possible that …?
- ❖ How did it come about that …?
- ❖ How did you happen to …?
- ❖ To what do you attribute …?

- **Minimize negative information**. Make it easy for the candidate to share things from their past experience that isn't so favorable. Offer sympathetic remarks that will make the candidate feel understood by you rather than judged. As soon as you react negatively, either verbally or nonverbally, to what a candidate has said, you will not get the person to open up again to give you the details you need. Please bear in mind, however, the nature of the unfavorable element. If, for example, someone shares with you that they have trouble being as assertive as they think they should be, offer a sympathetic remark. But, for matters of a more serious nature, it is not appropriate to offer these kinds of remarks. Impatience at working with others and instances of poor attendance, for example, should not be so casually dismissed. Address the issue by acknowledging it and giving the person credit for any means they have taken to address the problem.

Take the time to commit as many of the questions to memory as you can. This will aid the flow of the conversation and will prevent the candidate from feeling like he or she is being grilled.

Now that you've formulated your interview questions, let's explore other ways you can prepare for the interview.

Determine the Interview Method

Interviews, because of their very nature, have many forms. You can conduct a face-to-face interview with one person, with two people, with a team of people, via the phone, videoconferencing, and e-mail. While the face-to-face method is still the most common, the other mediums have merit as well.

- **Team Interviews.** These are more common for executive positions where Board members and other executives have a stake in the hiring decision. Many schools also use this approach when hiring new teachers or administrators— members from the Board, the administration, parent group, student group, and department join forces to get a feel for their candidate. Team interviews, however, can be very intimidating, so this format should be used for final-round interviewing only. Initial interviews can be conducted in a more informal way.

- **Telephone Interviews.** For initial interviews and screening, this is an economical and time-saving way of talking to candidates. While they should not take longer than 15 to 20 minutes, with proper preparation, a lot of information can be shared in that limited amount of time since candidates are sometimes more at ease in their home environment. Gather the information you need and either offer an invitation to come interview formally with your organization or thank them for their time. If you know at the time a candidate will not be asked for another interview, tell them you appreciate their interest but that you do not believe they would be a proper fit for the position. Ask them if you may keep their information on file for consideration for other positions that may open up in your organization. Always remember that you could be talking to an excellent candidate for another position, and you want that person to leave the conversation with a favorable impression of you and your organization.

- **Videoconferencing.** This can save in costly and time-consuming travel expenses, but it's really only feasible if both sites are equipped with the technological capability. Determine ahead of time if this is an option, particularly within an organization that has offices across the country.

- **E-mail**. Because this means of communication is so widespread and popular, this could be an excellent way for you to conduct initial interviews. While it is good for gathering information to decide if you would like to talk to the candidate again, it does not give you much information in the way of nonverbal communication. Decide what works for you and your initial screening process to see if this is a viable option for you. Using this method is contingent upon the candidate being technologically savvy, so be sure to have an alternate plan.

The rest of this book gives you tools to conduct a face-to-face interview because it is still the most popular method of interviewing. If you choose to incorporate other methods, take the ideas presented here and modify them to fit your needs and the interview medium.

Prepare Your Interview Location

The environment you create can have a positive or negative effect on the candidate. Choose the location carefully and pay attention to the details that will make the interview experience more pleasant for you and the candidate.

- Choose a well-ventilated room and adjust the temperature to accommodate conditions that are either too hot or too cold.

- Choose a location that is well lit, preferably with a window for an open, airy feeling.

- Eliminate clutter from flat surfaces.

- Create an interview area that does not position you to be across a table from a candidate. Opt to sit on the same side of the table to prevent any physical barriers to the conversation.

- Have glasses of water handy for both you and the candidate.

- Provide a hanger for the candidate's coat if the weather is cold.

- Take care of any distractions—turn off your cell phone, discourage phone calls being forwarded to your office, prevent entry to your office with an "In Conference" sign on your door.

- Appoint a person to meet, greet, and guide the candidate to the interview location.

- Have your list of questions ready and waiting.

- Have copies of any information you might provide the candidate about the position, your organization, etc.

Since you have planned everything to this point, do not overlook these details that will help you and the candidates relax and enjoy the conversation you are about to have.

Legal Issues You Should Consider

As mentioned earlier, asking job applicants certain kinds of questions is illegal and, therefore, harmful to your organization. Questions that deal with age, sex, marital status, ethnic origin, religious preference, sexual preference, or disabilities should never be asked. Federal legislation prohibits hiring decisions that are based on anything but the occupational requirements the position requires.

Here are some key legislative actions that affect the workplace:

- The Civil Rights legislation passed in 1964 prohibits discrimination based on race, color, religion, sex, or nation origin.

- The Age Discrimination Act (ADEA) prohibits employers from discriminating against workers who are over the age of 40. There are specific guidelines in this legislation for benefit, pension, and retirement plans.

- The Americans with Disabilities Act (ADA) protects individuals with disabilities who are otherwise able to execute the duties of the job. Modifications to the workplace may need to be done to address the individual's needs, but performance standards need not be affected.

Here are some examples of questions you should not ask:

- Do you live by yourself?
- When did you graduate from college?
- Do you already have childcare, or would you use the facility here in the building?
- Do you require single or family insurance coverage?
- Do you have any health problems?
- Is English your primary language?
- Do you have a significant other or partner that will need to relocate with you?
- Do you have a disability?
- What religious group do you belong to?
- Are you a member of the **** church?
- Have you ever been denied health insurance?
- Do you know my daughter? I think she is your age.
- Where were you when Kennedy was shot?
- Where were you when Challenger exploded?
- Will you be attending a class reunion any time soon?
- Are you a member of gay or lesbian organizations?

Questions You Should Ask

If there is a specific requirement of the job, you may ask questions about it. For example, if the job requires the employee to lift and carry heavy boxes, you may not ask if the candidate has a disability or health condition that would prevent that, but you may ask,

> *"This job requires you to lift 20 boxes per day, each weighing approximately 40 pounds. Would this be a problem for you?"*

Or, if the job requires night hours, you may not ask if the employee has a family at home, but you may ask,

> *"The hours of this position are from 11 p.m. to 7 a.m. Would this be a problem for you?"*

Some seemingly harmless questions can actually be based on discriminatory issues, so always check with your legal counsel or compliance department when in doubt. A good rule of thumb is to always carefully examine the needs of the position, and tailor your questions that ask for information on the candidate's ability to do the job, and nothing else.

Top 5 Ideas from this Chapter

- Use information from the job analysis to create behavioral interview questions.

- Take time to reflect, plan, and write down the interview questions as they pertain to the needs of the position.

- Take time to become familiar with the kinds of questions to ask and the strategies you can use to get the best information from your candidates.

- Determine the best format and location for your interview.

- Always be aware of federal legislation and guidelines when formulating questions for your candidates.

Chapter Four:
Conduct the Interview

Chapter Objectives

This chapter covers strategies to help you:

- ➤ Conduct effective, objective interviews.
- ➤ Establish rapport.
- ➤ Control your emotions during the interview.
- ➤ Ask questions and follow-up questions about past performance.
- ➤ Provide silence or wait time.
- ➤ Seek contrary evidence.
- ➤ Incorporate on-site performance.
- ➤ Understand the value of documentation.

You are as prepared as you can be; now it's time for action. Remember that the focus of the interview is the person's ability to DO the job not to GET the job. The following section will help you to prevent some of the biases that may enter in to your hiring decision.

Establish Rapport

As mentioned in Chapter 3, establishing rapport is a critical first step to a successful interview. The candidate should be made to feel welcome and comfortable and at ease. Because you are asking the individual to think about specifics as they pertain to the job, a relaxed candidate will be able to give you the information you need. Also by establishing rapport, you have effectively raised the candidate's opinion of you and your organization. If not hired for this position, he or she might be willing to consider a position with you again after having a positive interview experience.

One of the fastest and most effective ways of creating rapport with a candidate is to incorporate his or her name into the conversation whenever possible and appropriate. People love to be addressed by their names, and when handled respectfully and professionally, they, by nature, will respond favorably. Another way to build rapport is by finding something in the candidate's past experiences or on the application to which you can relate in some way. You could open the conversation by saying:

- Good morning, Deidra. I hope you found our offices without any difficulty. In preparing for your interview, I reviewed your resume once again and noticed that you started your career by participating in an archaeological dig. I have always been fascinated by that field and took a class when I was in college. Tell me, what was it like?

- Welcome, Shae. When we spoke on the phone last week, you mentioned that you were a member of the International Association of Financial Planners. I am too! Were you able to attend the national conference last month?

Take the time to plan what you will do specifically to create rapport with the candidate to create a comfortable, conversational environment.

Control Your Emotions

This is one of the most overlooked factors in the hiring process. In order to make a fair, effective, and objective decision, the emotions of the hiring manager must remain in check. Ask questions and uncover details that deal with the candidate's ability to do the job, not the personality and communication styles he or she prefers. Many hiring managers pride themselves on being able to tell as soon as someone enters the room if they are qualified for the position or not. Fundamental hiring mistakes can happen when the hiring manager sees, prefers, and hires in his or her own image. This is terribly unfair to the candidate, and unwise from a business perspective. You could pass right over the perfect person with assumptions and judgments such as these. Do not let your own agenda, biases, or preferences enter into this process—they have no place. It does not matter if you "click" with the person. What does matter is his or her ability to do the job and what talents and abilities the individual can add to your organization.

Here are some tips to help you remain as objective as possible:

- Reject first impressions—they are often misleading and based on emotions, stereotyping, biases, style, or chemistry.

- Talk to yourself throughout the interview to remain objective.

- Avoid making decisions too soon. You require time to find out all of the details you need to know. The more you dig for information, the more data you have to support your decision. The more data you have about a candidate's past performance, the more likely you are to make informed hiring decisions. You are also less likely to base your decisions on subjective elements.

- Realize that some of the negative traits you might be witnessing could be directly related to nervousness. Most people loosen up and feel less nervous as the interview progresses. Do not automatically interpret such traits as slow responses, no eye contact, lack of warmth or confidence negatively. It could very well just be stage fright.

- Be sure to follow your pre-determined questions. This will eliminate the tendency to judge the candidate on anything other than the work and his or her capability to execute it.

- Listen more than you talk. You will collect more evidence of past performance if you tune in and listen to every word. The candidate should speak about 85 percent of the time you have together.

- Be the devil's advocate. If all you are hearing and perceiving are things that appear only positive, or vice versa, reserve judgment at all costs. There has to be a flip side—your job is to find it!

Ask Questions and Follow-Up Questions About Past Job Performance

This is where you utilize all of the questions you formulated from Chapter 3. Focus on past job performance and probe for the details you need to make a good match. Throughout the interview, you are looking for clues as to how this person performed in similar tasks, how successful they were, and the specifics to support them. You can begin the conversation with something like:

*"Jay, tell me about your present job at IT
Specialists."*

You can now follow up with a more specific
question, such as:

*"You indicated that you had the responsibility
to train employees new to the program your
organization uses. Tell me about your role as
a trainer and leader."*

You may now use probing questions to flush
out the details:

*"What specific training strategies did you use
in your classes?"*

*"Think of a situation where these strategies
were not as effective. Describe in detail what
you did to help that employee learn the
program?"*

As you practice using these techniques, questions, follow-up questions, and probing for more
detail will become second nature. If you keep your
focus on redirecting questions until you get the
specifics you need, you will have conducted a
successful behavioral interview.

A last note on gathering information: stay in
control of the conversation. Some candidates may
stray from the original question and talk at great
length about things that have no bearing on the
interview or the job in question. Others may want to
start asking you questions before you have the

information you need or want. It is your job to rein the individual in. Be polite, but firm, inform the candidate that there will be time allowed for his or her questions later in the interview, and redirect the conversation back to its original course. An example of staying in control of the conversation is:

> *"That is a good question; I'm glad you have questions about the position and the organization. We will have time in just a few minutes to address them, but at this time I would like to return to some of the details you were explaining about your latest project."*

Allow Silence or Wait Time

We, as humans, are not generally comfortable with lulls or silence in a conversation, particularly in such a structured conversation as an interview. This time is crucial to the respondent, however. Since many candidates may not be as prepared as they could be, or are trying to recall specifics from job performance, this silence is bound to happen at some point. If you are looking for thoughtful, specific answers to your questions, many of which may be complex, do not expect or even desire a ready answer. Encourage the candidate to take the time he or she needs to reflect and phrase an answer.

> *"Take all the time you need, Bill. Sometimes it takes a moment of thought to apply these questions to your experience."*

"Don't worry, Carol. Take a moment to compose your thoughts—we'll resume when you are ready."

Many candidates find that these phrases give them permission to relax and to think in order to respond. The time they need to take may actually decrease since they are not worried about the silence their thinking creates.

Seek Contrary Evidence

Because many of our hiring decisions are based on first impressions or emotional responses, we tend to ask questions that will continue to confirm our initial findings. This is another reason why remaining objective in an interview situation is crucial to good hiring decisions.

There are many courses, books, and organizations dedicated to preparing people to interview. Information on how to dress, courtesies to extend, questions that might be asked, good answers to those questions, etc., are covered in detail. Consequently, you may have a very slick, articulate candidate in front of you with all of the "right" answers to your questions. Seeking contrary evidence will help you to discover the areas where this candidate may need some work. If all of the situations and details the candidate has given you so far are positive, specifically ask for situations or details that did not work out so positively.

For example:

*"Mary, you've given me a great deal of good,
specific information. Now I would like you to
tell me about an instance when the business
system you created did not work. What hap-
pened, and what were the effects?"*

*"Dawn, I asked earlier about a time when you
needed to analyze the training program in your
organization. I need to revisit that again
because I do not feel the question was com-
pletely answered."*

Conversely, seeking contrary evidence also
helps you to remain objective when all of the information has been negative. Have the answers really
been negative, or is it your perception of them
because of different personality traits or communication styles? Ask questions that might help you to
gain a better understanding of the candidate and his
or her abilities to perform on the job.

*"Bob, we've discussed a few incidents where
things did not go as planned. Take a moment to
tell me about a time that you were proud of
what you accomplished on the job, and why.
Give me as many specific details as you can
about the situation."*

Approach each interview with the understanding that every candidate has positive and negative
experiences or attributes, and you are there to dis-

cover what they are. This, again, represents good behavioral interviewing.

On-site Performance

Decide ahead of time if you would like to have the candidate actually perform a key function of the position to help you assess his or her ability to transfer skills. There are any number of tasks you can have them complete; be sure to give them enough advance notice if they should need to provide you with anything upon their arrival.

Here are some ideas:

- Have the candidates provide you with a portfolio of specific examples of past work that aligns with the objectives of the job.

- Have the candidate give a presentation about a pre-determined topic or process.

- If you have a design project, give candidates the parameters of the project, and ask them how they would create a solution.

- Give a managerial candidate the overall structure of the department, current challenges impeding progress, and invite the candidate to draw up an action plan.

There are any number of possibilities this affords. Two good rules of thumb, however, are to make sure you have enough time (you could, perhaps, give candidates until the next day to submit their plans/ideas) and to be sure what you are asking them to do directly correlates with the position for which they are interviewing. This provides a wonderful opportunity to see if the candidate can perform the tasks required of the position.

Review Performance Expectations

It is very important that the candidate have a good understanding of what the position entails and what the performance expectations are. Review the job analysis and job description with each person so that they can make an informed decision.

Allow for Questions

Toward the end of the interview, invite the candidate to ask any questions he or she might have. The kinds of questions or lack of questions can give you a lot of information regarding the candidate's level of interest, motivation, aptitude for the job, and knowledge base. Pay careful attention and answer the questions as thoroughly and accurately as you can.

Take Notes

This is something many hiring managers do not do, or do not do sufficiently. It will be impossible after the interview to recall everything that was said without accurate, thorough notes taken at the time. Without specific notes, one tends to remember the overall impression of the interview, which again can be based on biases or judgments. For each of the questions asked, write down the response. This will also help you determine during the course of the interview if sufficient behavioral examples have been given for each question asked. You can always return to that point if you are not satisfied with the amount of information you have written down.

One way to do this is to use the template that you have already created (see pages 103–106).

At the end of the interview, review your notes and write down any summary remarks that you would like to make at that time. This would also be a good time to note the questions that the candidate asked. But please, do not decide at this point if someone will or will not get the position—this takes careful consideration after all of the candidates have had a fair and impartial interview.

Notes from Interview

Candidate's Name:					
Criteria	**Details to Support** **Skills and Experience**				
Core Area					
Core Area					
Core Area					
Core Area					

Continued . . .

Motivation			
	Eagerness for more responsibility	Willingness to work	Commitment to lifelong learning

Continued . . .

Ability to Add Value/Apply Experience			
Ability to create opportunity			
Quality of work			
Ability to transfer skills and knowledge			

Continued . . .

Aptitude	
	Aptitude for critical thinking/problem solving

Top 5 Ideas from this Chapter

- Establishing rapport will create an environment in which the candidate will talk freely about past job performance.

- Train yourself to remain objective throughout the entire interview and avoid making any decisions or judgments before you have all the evidence.

- Ask, follow up, and probe for details of past job performance throughout the interview.

- During the interview, find examples of contrary evidence to balance out your overall picture of the candidate.

- Consider incorporating on-site performance elements into your interview, if it is suitable to the position and to time constraints.

Chapter Five: Evaluate, Select, and Make the Offer

Chapter Objectives

This chapter covers strategies to help you:

- ➢ Check all references.
- ➢ Compile assessment information.
- ➢ Formulate and analyze all data.
- ➢ Identify warning signs from potential candidates.
- ➢ Make the decision on whom to hire.
- ➢ Make the offer.
- ➢ Notify other candidates.

Now that the interviews are completed, it is time to evaluate and make a decision on whom to hire. This takes careful analysis of all of the elements that factor in to your hiring decision. Take the time to establish a system you can use to compare candidates' strengths and abilities.

Check All References

If you haven't already done this before the interview, now is the time. Contact the references provided by the candidate and obtain as much information as you can about the duration of the candidate's employment, his or her job title, and anything else the employer is willing to provide. For many organizations, this is the extent of the information they are prepared or willing to share. However, asking the following questions may yield important information to help you make the final decision.

- In what capacity do you know this person?

- How long have you been acquainted?

- In your opinion, what are this person's greatest strengths?

- How did this person progress during his or her time with you?

- In your opinion, how did the organization benefit from having had this person as an employee?

- Is this person welcome or eligible to be re-hired by your organization?

- Is there anything else you can share that will help me in this matter?

Take the information gathered from these discussions and include them in your final review. A hiring rubric is included later in the chapter and provides a place for your reference check findings.

Compile Assessment Information

Employees and applicants vary widely in their knowledge, skills, abilities, interests, work styles, and other characteristics. These differences systematically affect the way people perform or behave on the job. Organizations that have identified or benchmarked work-related characteristics associated with job success often use assessment tools to measure a candidate's fit for the job.

There are many types of employment-related assessment tools used for different purposes:

Selection

Organizations want to be able to identify and hire the best people for the job and the organization in a fair and efficient manner. A properly developed assessment tool may provide a way to select successful salespeople, concerned customer service representatives, and effective workers in many other occupations.

Placement

Organizations also want to be able to assign people to the appropriate job level. For example, an organization may have several managerial positions, each having a different level of responsibility. Assessment may provide information that helps organizations achieve the best fit between employees and jobs.

Training and Development

Tests are used to find out whether employees have mastered training materials. They can help identify those applicants and employees who might benefit from either remedial or advanced training. Information gained from testing can be used to design or modify training programs. Test results also help individuals identify areas in which self-development activities would be useful.

Promotion

Organizations may use tests to identify employees who possess managerial potential or higher level capabilities so that these employees can be promoted to assume greater duties and responsibilities.

The number of laws and regulations governing the employment process has increased over the past four decades. Many of these laws and regulations have important implications for conducting employment assessment. One set of standards that employers and organizations will want to follow when choosing assessment tools for hiring and selection is the *Uniform Guidelines on Employee Selection Procedures,* published by the Federal Equal Employment Opportunity Commission (EEOC).

Using a single test or procedure will provide you with a limited view of a person's employment qualifications. Moreover, you may reach a mistaken conclusion by giving too much weight to a single test result. On the other hand, using a variety of assessment tools enables you to get a more complete picture of the individual. The practice of using a variety of tests and procedures to more fully assess people is referred to as the *whole-person approach* to employment-based assessment. The TotalView Assessment, distributed by Training House, illustrates this recommended *whole-person approach* to measuring work-related characteristics. This one-hour assessment provides standardized performance scores on four ability measures, including a measure of general ability, 24 personality dimensions, and three motivation/interest scales. For more information on the TotalView Assessment, see Appendix B.

Properly used, employment-related assessment can reveal valuable information that may not be discovered during the course of a typical interview. Prior to selecting assessment tools, engaging a consultant with expertise in employment-related assessment may be helpful in choosing the right assessments to use for measuring specific job characteristics.

Formulate and Analyze All Data

Now that you've gathered your reference check and assessment information, it is time to review and evaluate your candidates. Because there is so much information for each candidate, it makes the process much easier for the hiring manager if the data is organized for each person. The following rubric is just one example of how you can lay out the information from the interview. By having a uniform table for each candidate, you can streamline the comparison of data and can also prevent key omissions.

The criteria established here is arbitrary—please customize it to fit your specific needs. Refer back to the specific skills needed to execute the job and your interview questions to come up with the criteria for each position.

Hiring Rubric

Candidate's Name:

Criteria	Very Good	Adequate	Poor	Details to Support
Skills and Experience				
Core Area				
Core Area				
Core Area				
Core Area				

Continued . . .

Criteria	Very Good	Adequate	Poor	Details to Support
Motivation				
Eagerness for more responsibility				
Willingness to work				
Commitment to lifelong learning				

Continued . . .

Criteria	Very Good	Adequate	Poor	Details to Support
Ability to add value/apply experience				
Ability to create opportunity				
Quality of work				
Ability to transfer skills and knowledge				

Continued . . .

Criteria	Very Good	Adequate	Poor	Details to Support
Aptitude				
Aptitude for critical thinking/problem solving				
References				
Comments from Reference 1				
Comments from Reference 2				
Comments from Reference 3				
Assessments or on-site performance elements				

Identify Warning Signs from Potential Candidates

After your chart is completed for each person, add to it somewhere any warning signs that may have emerged during your information gathering. These may come from references or the candidates themselves, but they demand careful scrutiny. It is also advisable and appropriate to allow the candidates a chance to clarify or refute any discrepancies that are found in this process. Here are some possible warning signs:

- The candidate is late to the interview and does not offer an explanation.

- The information provided on the resume or discovered during the interview reveals that the candidate did not list jobs between the ones on the resume.

- The candidate's background reveals frequent job changes.

- Circumstances around why the candidate left a certain position remains unclear or was negative.

- The candidate cannot provide adequate references, or you are unable to verify them.

- The candidate seems overly concerned with work hour requirements or compensation.

- The assessment identifies some core area or cognitive skill that is not in line with the needs of the position.

While none of these alone constitutes grounds for a negative decision, they do merit careful consideration and further fact-finding.

Talk to other hiring managers within or outside your organization to determine other possible warning signs they have encountered over the years.

Warning Signs Other Hiring Managers Have Encountered

Additional Warning Signs	Source
1.	
2.	
3.	
4.	
5.	
6.	
7.	
8.	

Make the Decision on Whom to Hire

The facts are in, everything has been reviewed and evaluated; it is now time to make a decision. If your notes from the interviews were detailed enough, you were able to fill in your hiring criteria chart with little difficulty. Take the charts from your top candidates and compare them.

- Which candidate will best be able to fill the needs of the position?

- Which candidate will be best equipped to take this position to the next level?

- Which candidate will be willing and able to adapt to change?

- Which candidate will be the greatest asset to the future of the department and the organization?

- Which candidate will best be able to apply previously acquired skills to this new position?

- Which candidate has the necessary skills?

Asking yourself questions such as these will help you evaluate the candidates. Always remember to keep subjective elements out of this decision; the answers to your behavioral-based questions and all other data uncovered should be the basis for your final decision.

If others will be participating in the final evaluation, make record of each person's assessment and recommendation for employment. Use the form on page 122.

When you have made your decision, write a brief paragraph about each of the final candidates. This helps in crystallizing your final assessment, gives a clear-cut rationale as to why one candidate was chosen over another, and gives you a chance to recommend this candidate for other positions in the organization for which they may be better suited. Do not let the wish to see this person in another department preclude the consideration for this position, however. Use the forms on pages 123 and 124.

Recommendation for Employment

Candidate	Reviewer 1	Reviewer 2	Reviewer 3	Reviewer 4
Candidate #1				
Candidate #2				
Candidate #3				

Candidate Name: _____

This candidate was recommended for hire because:

_____

_____

_____

_____

_____

_____

_____

_____

_____

_____

_____

_____

_____

_____

_____

_____

_____

_____

Candidate Name: _____

This candidate was not recommended for hire because:

_____

_____

_____

_____

_____

_____

_____

_____

_____

_____

_____

_____

_____

_____

_____

_____

_____

_____

Make the Offer

As soon as the decision has been made, notify the chosen candidate and extend an offer of employment. While it is important to give the hiring process and consideration adequate and thorough time, you do not want it to drag out any longer than it needs to. With such a demand for employees these days, a slow offer could result in a missed opportunity if another organization has extended an offer before yours.

When making a job offer, be sure you don't make promises that you can't keep. For example, avoid things like, "Bob, it's great to have you on board. I'm sure you'll be manager within a year," and other such statements that could compromise you later.

It is typical to call the individual and inform him or her of your decision. Offer the position and wait for a response. If the candidate needs time to consider your offer, by all means give them several days to do so. If there is a serious time constraint, inform the candidate that a response within the next 48 hours would help you to meet demands.

If the candidate accepts, verbalize the agreement over the phone and formalize it in writing the same day, complete with any compensation or benefit plan information. Be sure to detail the start date of the position, the hour to report, and to whom to report. Mail the new hire's copy or have him or her come to the organization to sign any necessary paperwork.

Notify Other Candidates

Wait to notify the other candidates until your first choice has accepted. If the person declines, you still have time to reconsider the other candidates who also demonstrated the appropriate skills and abilities.

During the interview process, be sure to notify the applicants who will not be receiving invitations to interview. This, while disappointing to the person, is much better than not hearing anything at all from your organization. It is always important to maintain the integrity and reputation of your business to members of the community, and this is a prime opportunity to do so. Explain that while they will not be considered for this position, their information will remain on file for one year for consideration for other positions that come open.

To those candidates who did receive interviews but not the position, the same diplomacy applies. Notify each with a professional letter that thanks them for their time and interest they have offered your organization. Explain that while they did exhibit many of the skills and qualifications necessary for the job, another candidate was chosen at this time. Again, tell them that their resume and information will remain on file for one year to be considered for other positions. Try to give this letter a personal note of some kind. Address them by name in the letter, and let them know that you truly enjoyed speaking with them in the interview and wish them luck in their endeavors. A few well-chosen and sincere words will go a long way in maintaining their good opinions of you and the organization.

Top 5 Ideas from this Chapter

- Thorough reference checks can give you information to either confirm or deny information uncovered in the interview.

- Aptitude tests also provide a great deal of information in addition to the interview if EEOC guidelines and legislation are closely adhered to.

- Detail, in chart form, all of the data and examples you collect from each candidate for easy and consistent review.

- Tune in to, and clarify, any warning signs from the candidate.

- Once an offer has been made and accepted, notify all other applicants and interviewees of your decision.

Chapter Six:
Orient and Retain
Your Employees

Chapter Objectives

This chapter covers strategies to help you:

➤ Implement orientation strategies.
➤ Retain your employees.
➤ Use motivation and recognition techniques.

Congratulations! You've worked hard and invested a lot of time and resources into finding and hiring the right person for the job. Now it's time to focus on your strategy to keeping your employee through high job satisfaction. This chapter will give you some ideas on how to start your employee off right and keep and maintain his or her job satisfaction.

You might feel relieved at this point—you've done a good job. But really, your work is just beginning. In Chapter 1, we discussed what a good hire can mean to an organization and just how expensive employee turnover can be. Review the dollar amount you came up with for one instance of employee turnover. Always keep this in mind, and constantly work to keep your employees challenged and satisfied.

Orientation Strategies

One of the first things you can do to ensure employee satisfaction is implement an employee-friendly orientation program. Keep in mind that changing jobs is a stressful time, and many people might not be very relaxed the first few days of a new job.

Consider staggering the information you need to provide the employee over a few weeks. For example, on the first day, make sure they know what to do and to whom to report, and give them a tour of the area or organization. Most people at this point are wondering how to use the phone system, where the restrooms are, and how to navigate the cafeteria at noon—the fundamentals. Take this into account and make them as comfortable as possible without overwhelming them the first day.

Over the course of the next few days or weeks, continue to spend time with them to help them acclimate to the organization's culture, specific pro-cedures, and how their job connects with other departments to benefit the organization. You will find your new employee will feel less stressed by the transition and will forge a closer relationship with you in the process. This is good. The more you spend time with and get to know your people, the better able you are to ensure their happiness on the job.

Here are some ideas to make your new employee feel special and welcome at your organization:

Welcome Your New Employee

- Have a co-worker in the same department meet the new employee at the door. This might also be the same person you assign to be his or her mentor for the first few weeks. It helps to have someone specially designated to answer questions.

- Have a special parking place for the new employee to use during the first few weeks.

- Invite the new employee out to lunch with yourself and the president or COO of the organization.

- Encourage the new person's department members to invite the new person to lunch each day of the first week.

- Take the time to give him or her a thorough tour of the facility.

- Introduce the new employee to the people they can contact with needs or concerns.

- Introduce and welcome the new employee at departmental or organization-wide meetings.

- Be sure the new person has all of the materials necessary. Tell them who to contact for resources when the need arises.

- After the first month of employment, have a brief discussion with the employee to see how effective the transition was. Find out what worked and what could have helped the new employee even more. This is valuable feedback to hone and perfect your orientation time for new employees in the future.

Remember

Review again the expectations that were drawn out during the interview process. It is essential that during the first week of employment you schedule a meeting to discuss expectations. Tell new employees what you expect them to do, how to do it (if certain procedures are required), and how and to whom to report. Setting down these expectations and clarifying any concerns or questions employees might have at this point will go a long way to increasing employee satisfaction.

Keep Your Employees

I hear of many employers who are hesitant to incorporate very simple strategies to keep employees into their overall plan because they are afraid of all the cost and effort it will take. Many also feel that those costs would be in vain because employees will eventually leave anyway. You can see how this attitude contradicts success! By not exerting every effort to keep good employees, you will almost certainly lose them.

The following tips will help you make it hard for good people to look elsewhere!

Tips for Retaining Employees

Pay Fairly

This does not mean you have to top the market you are in, but you should definitely be above the average for each position. Get feedback from employees about their satisfaction with the benefits you provide, and modify if necessary. Check area businesses to ensure your benefits offered are competitive.

Analyze Environment

Be aware of the environment you create in your organization. What are you doing to make working at your organization a pleasant and enjoyable experience? Look at your company as though you're seeing it for the first time. Check for evidence of the following things:

- Open lines of communication
- A clean, safe, and pleasant physical environment
- Responsive policies to accommodate employees' home lives
- A regular opportunity to have fun
- Sincere appreciation for employees

Promote Your Mission

More than anything people need to know that what they do makes a difference. They need to believe that their work is worthwhile and significant. Show them how they add to the value of the organization, and be clear on what the organization stands for and is trying to accomplish.

Involve and Empower

Innovation in today's market is essential. You never know where the best ideas will come from. Listen to your employees. They have many ideas on how to get things done more creatively, quickly, and profitably. Our workforce today is more educated and mobile. This means that they have learned a lot from other companies and might see a way to streamline your organization. To reach your potential as an organization, tap into the minds of your own employees. Encourage their ideas and the expression of them openly. Also, by encouraging, incorporating, and appropriately crediting the idea to the employee, you will create an environment of trust and teamwork.

Allow for Errors

Make room for mistakes. If people are afraid to make mistakes, they will be afraid to take risks—they'll stay in their comfort zones forever. If you do support learning and risk-taking, remind your employees of this. Humans are usually afraid of failure. Encourage employees to look at risk and growth as positive things. In this open atmosphere, creativity will prosper.

Understand Personal Needs

Treat your people very well. Pay attention to each person to determine what this means to them. Employees will have different needs at different times, and if you tune in and are aware of what they need or would appreciate most, you will establish a win-win relationship.

We spend a great deal of time figuring out and catering to our customers' needs—if we don't, they will go somewhere else. This is the same philosophy you should have about your employees. It's hard to leave an organization that truly has your individual needs at heart!

Understand Professional Needs

Tune in to your employees' professional needs as well. Schedule regular reviews of the employee's progress. We've gotten into the habit of thinking of reviews as annual salary reviews. Reviews to provide employees with valuable feedback should not just be an annual event—they should be a regular occurrence. This is also an excellent opportunity to address or offer any training needs the employee needs or wants. Review the core areas and trait areas with them, and determine together where the training time should be spent. Employees need this time to check in on their progress, review expectations, and set professional goals. Be a coach in these situations. Collaborate with them. Enable them to shape their own work, not just do their job.

Observing the employee can give you a lot of information about their professional satisfaction. If you observe behaviors or nonverbal clues that indicate dissatisfaction, try to find out why.

- **Do they need more of a challenge?**
  Assign a special project, or have them train new employees in the department.

- **Do they have all of the skills they need?**
  Assess skills and recommend appropriate intervention.

- **Do they seem bored by routine?**
  Consider varying job assignment within a department. This keeps everyone fresh and aware of what's going on in other areas.

- **Are they properly matched with the job?**
  Even through our best efforts, sometimes employees are placed inappropriately. Find out their strengths and put them in a position to capitalize on those strengths. You will have a satisfied employee and a stronger business.

You will find these ideas very simple in nature, but profoundly powerful in practice. Use them. Incorporate them into your business strategy and perfect them to meet your special requirements.

Motivation and Recognition Techniques

You can spend as much or as little money as you like on recognition tools. What's the key to effective rewards? Sincerity. People respond to and flourish given prompt and sincere recognition and praise. They will become resentful if a reward or thank you is perceived as superficial and, therefore, meaningless. Work on a system for rewards within your organization, and remain faithful and consistent to it. Remember, though, that the more tools you have to provide recognition, the better your chances

of finding the perfect thing for each employee.
Reward by giving what is meaningful to the employee. People have a tendency to work harder and
smarter when there is something in it for them. In
order to make these programs effective, employees
need to be motivated by them. To do this, keep in
mind the following four tips that will help you to
create a good program:

1. **Tie rewards to specific employee needs**.
   The flexibility this provides will help you
   reward your good employees in ways that
   are meaningful to them.

2. **Present rewards regularly and publicly**. If
   the presentation is camouflaged as a staff
   meeting, the value will decrease. Also, by
   having presentations frequently you ensure
   that recognition is given in a timely fashion.

3. **Promote the value of the reward**. If
   managers talk favorably about the reward/
   award and what it means, it inherently
   becomes more valuable.

4. **Promote, but don't oversell**. If too much
   emphasis is placed on the reward/award, the
   meaning of it will be lowered and discussion
   will verge on the ridiculous.

A recognition program will grow and evolve as
your organization does, so be sure to revisit it
frequently to ensure its effectiveness and vitality.

Make it fun for you and your employees! After all, you can't beat recognition and fun in the same event!

Here is a list of ideas for you to help make your reward program fun and interesting. Find the one(s) that best suit you and your employees.

- Write a personal note in your own hand-writing to employees who are doing a great job.

- Encourage other employees to send notes or other tokens of recognition to someone they appreciate and why.

- Send flowers on birthdays or employment anniversaries.

- Provide employees with "wearables" such as organization T-shirts, caps, buttons, sweatshirts, etc.

- Treat employees and their spouses to dinner for a job well done.

- Allocate special parking to the employee who made the biggest difference during the previous month of business.

- Display a "Wall of Honor" and have pictures of outstanding employees, and what their contributions were.

- When certain goals are met, allow a "casual day."

- Designate days once a month when employees can come in late.

- Have departments nominate and vote on their Most Valuable Player.

- Give magazine subscriptions.

- Set up recognition luncheons.

- Provide time for group events, such as departmental golf outings.

- Offer:

    - ❖ Health club memberships.

    - ❖ Training sessions and location of the employee's choice.

    - ❖ Pay raise or bonus.

    - ❖ Promotion.

    - ❖ Better sales territory.

    - ❖ Toys or events for the employee's child(ren).

    - ❖ Dinner out with the boss.

    - ❖ Limousine ride to work for a week.

    - ❖ Gift baskets of specialty foods.

    - ❖ Items that complement an employee's hobbies or outside interests.

    - ❖ Subscription to Internet service.

❖ Tickets to events or sneak-preview movies.

❖ Gift certificates to local shops or for services.

❖ Books, tapes, or videos.

❖ Tote bags, briefcases, laptop carry cases.

❖ Free gourmet lunch on the spot.

❖ Electronic devices.

❖ Personalized items with the organization logo and employee name. For example, coffee mugs, pens or other office items.

❖ Lottery tickets.

❖ Shares of organization stock.

❖ Weekend trips for employee and family.

❖ Department "retreats."

• Hire an assistant for the most productive sales representative.

• Write articles in the organization newsletter dedicated to recognizing employee efforts.

• Hire a service to help the employee with personal chores, such as a maid service, a babysitting service, a lawn service, etc.

- Submit names of outstanding employees to local newspapers or industry trade magazines, specifying what the employee did and how it added value to the organization and the community.

- Provide regular training and discussion sessions.

- Sponsor organization cookouts. Nothing is more fun than food!

- Create certificates of recognition and present them publicly.

- Have a surprise party for an employee who has made a difference.

- Provide awards to people with good attendance, longevity with the organization, etc.

As you can see, there is no lack of inspiration when it comes to finding the right reward for your employees. Use this to your benefit, and you will have a successful program!

Throughout this book, we have discussed how to find, hire, and retain top employees. Take the ideas in this book to create your hiring system and process, and revisit it in 6 to 12 months to see how you are doing. Learn from the mistakes, refine your understanding of the concepts presented here, and hiring success can be yours!

Top 5 Ideas from this Chapter

- Maintaining employees in your organization takes concerted effort and a plan.

- Set up and clarify your organization's orientation plan for new employees.

- Follow the tips for keeping good people.

- Have motivation and recognition strategies to reward good performance.

- Be sincere in all dealings with employees, especially praise.

Appendix A:
Tools and Templates

Turnover Costs Worksheet

Source	Expense
1. Recruiting costs/advertising	$
2. Time to screen applicants.	$
3. Time to interview applicants.	$
4. Time and resources to train new person.	$
5. Loss of productivity to learning curve.	$
6. Loss of productivity of others who "pick up the slack" in the transition.	$
7. Moving costs to relocate new hire	$
8.	$
9.	$
10.	$
11.	$
12.	$
Total Cost for One Employee Turnover =	$

Costs – Improperly Placed Employees

Ineffective Element	Effect on Organization	Short-Term	Long-Term			
Turnover costs						
Low productivity						
Low morale						
Frustration of good employees						
Conflicts						
Poor customer service						

Continued . . .

Costs – Improperly Placed Employees

Ineffective Element	Effect on Organization	Short-Term	Long-Term		
Knowledge of job inadequate					
Ability to do job inadequate					
Willingness to do job inadequate					
Inappropriate behavior					
Inefficient use of resources					
Other:					

Hiring System Action Steps

Action Steps to Implement or Change Hiring System	Individuals/ Departments Involved	Completion Date
1.		
2.		
3.		
4.		
5.		

Continued . . .

Hiring System Action Steps

Action Steps to Implement or Change Hiring System	Individuals/ Departments Involved	Completion Date
6.		
7.		
8.		
9.		
10.		

Analyze Recruitment Methods

Recruitment Method	# New Hires Produced
1.	
2.	
3.	
4.	
5.	
6.	
7.	
8.	
9.	
10.	

Recruiting Action Plan

Recruitment Method	Timeline
1.	
2.	
3.	
4.	
5.	
6.	
7.	
8.	
9.	
10.	

Creating Behavioral Interview Questions

Preface statements or questions with:

- Provide an example of a time …
- Give an instance when …
- Tell me about a time …
- Describe an example …

Criteria	Details to Support
Skills and Experience	
Core Area: • •	• •
Core Area: • •	• •

Continued . . .

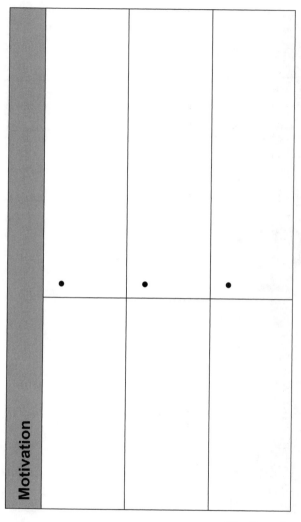

Motivation

Continued . . .

Ability to Add Value/Apply Experience

Continued . . .

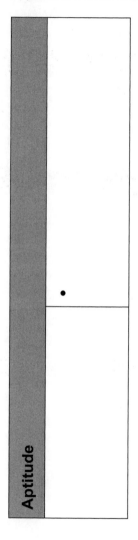

Aptitude

Kinds of Questions

Rapport-building
1.
2.
3.
Open-ended questions for past performance
1.
2.
3.
4.
5.
Probing/Follow-up questions
1.
2.
3.
4.
5.

Notes from Interview

Candidate's Name:					
Criteria	**Details to Support**				
Skills and Experience					
Core Area					
Core Area					
Core Area					
Core Area					

Continued . . .

Motivation			
Eagerness for more responsibility			
Willingness to work			
Commitment to lifelong learning			

Continued . . .

Ability to Add Value/Apply Experience			
Ability to create opportunity			
Quality of work			
Ability to transfer skills and knowledge			

Continued . . .

Aptitude
Aptitude for critical thinking/problem solving

Hiring Rubric

Candidate's Name:

Criteria	Very Good	Adequate	Poor	Details to Support
Skills and Experience				
Core Area				
Core Area				
Core Area				
Core Area				

Continued . . .

Criteria	Very Good	Adequate	Poor	Details to Support
Motivation				
Eagerness for more responsibility				
Willingness to work				
Commitment to lifelong learning				

Continued . . .

Criteria	Very Good	Adequate	Poor	Details to Support
Ability to add value/apply experience				
Ability to create opportunity				
Quality of work				
Ability to transfer skills and knowledge				

Continued . . .

Criteria	Very Good	Adequate	Poor	Details to Support
Aptitude				
Aptitude for critical thinking/problem solving				
References				
Comments from Reference 1				
Comments from Reference 2				
Comments from Reference 3				

Warning Signs Other Hiring Managers Have Encountered

Additional Warning Signs	Source
1.	
2.	
3.	
4.	
5.	
6.	
7.	
8.	

Recommendation for Employment

Candidate	Reviewer 1	Reviewer 2	Reviewer 3	Reviewer 4
Candidate #1				
Candidate #2				
Candidate #3				

Candidate Name: _____

This candidate was recommended for hire
because:

_____

_____

_____

_____

_____

_____

_____

_____

_____

_____

_____

_____

_____

_____

_____

_____

_____

Candidate Name: _____

This candidate was not recommended for
hire because:

_____

_____

_____

_____

_____

_____

_____

_____

_____

_____

_____

_____

_____

_____

_____

_____

_____

_____

Appendix B:
The *TotalView*™ Assessment

The TotalView Assessment is a precision psychometric tool used in the selection, coaching, and development of employees in any size business or organization. The construction and validation of the TotalView Assessment was completed by Dr. David Bartram, International R & D Director for the SHL Group plc., and current president of the International Test Commission. The TotalView was validated on a cross-cultural, multi-racial, and multi-lingual population of more than 4,700 employees representing the United States, Canada, Great Britain, Singapore, and Malaysia. Dr. Bartram's work has produced a world-class selection and development instrument that is valid, reliable, and culture-fair.

How the TotalView Assessment Works

The process begins with a candidate completing the TotalView Assessment, which measures Abilities, Interests, and Personality. The assessment can be administered by paper and pencil, by PC, or on the Internet.

The TotalView Assessment Software generates five reports that aid management in making human resource decisions. The reports graphically display the candidate's scores for each of the scales measured and provides an easy-to-read Total-Person narrative report. Figure 1 is an example of the selection report's graph, and Figure 2 is an example of the selection report's Total-Person narrative that discusses the candidate's fit for the job based on a validated job suitability benchmark or profile.

Figure 1. Example—
Selection Report Graph

Figure 2. Example—
Total-Person Narrative

Total Person
John Sample   Sales & Marketing Representative

Note:
The Total Person is a combination of all the elements Mr. John Sample completed in his TotalView Assessment.

Mr. John Sample has superior verbal skills, above average numeric skills, and average spatial skills. Assignments that involve reading and writing will be easiest for him. He should excel at any kind of paperwork or written material. Almost as adept with numbers as with words, he is also well able to do challenging numeric assignments such as working with complex spreadsheets and data tables. Because he is reasonably proficient in tasks that require mental manipulation of shapes and objects, he will be able to follow routine diagrams, to estimate space requirements, and to read blueprints.

Although Mr. Sample will need a little more time for tasks dependent on spatial reasoning, whenever he can use his exceptional skills in verbal or numeric reasoning, he will learn quickly and his job performance should be above average. John Sample will perform best when the environment and work practices change slowly.

Mr. Sample is strongly motivated to work with people and things, and moderately inclined to work with data. Regarding computer tasks, he would prefer direct communication with others via Internet connections, E-mail, and word processing. His average interest in information processing means that he would have to exert himself in any data management tasks and when doing detailed paperwork. Because he likes to work with others, he should do well in a position requiring social skills.

Mr. Sample is highly assertive and competitive. He willingly puts forth his own views, and has no fear of confrontation or controversy. In pursuit of his goals, he will show little concern for others and may be uncooperative with those who do not share his views. As a decisive leader, John Sample is driven to succeed and will work hard to reach his goals.

John Sample is reasonably well-organized, tidy, and accountable. Although he prefers to work in a structured environment, he is flexible and can be innovative if necessary. He prefers the status quo to change for change's sake. However, he can adapt quite readily and is not an obsessive planner. As long as changes are not seen as arbitrary or radical, he can cope with new developments. Mr. Sample can tolerate a relatively constant flow of routine tasks and still deal well with the occasional novelty.

TotalView Assessment Reports

1. Selection Report to assist with suggested job interview questions or hiring applications.

2. Coaching Report for training and coaching requirements.

3. Succession Planning Report to compare a candidate to various job Benchmarks or many candidates to one job Benchmark.

4. Individual Report that can be made available to permanent employees for development and coaching.

5. Working Characteristics Report provides information on five business-related behaviors.

What the TotalView Assessment Measures

The TotalView Assessment utilizes Sten scores. Sten means the standard tenth of a normal bell curve, as shown in Figure 3 below. This compares the items measured by the TotalView Assessment (Abilities, Interests, and Personality) with those of the general working population. The majority of people will score in the average 4–5–6–7 range, which constitutes 68% of the general working population. Scores in the far left or right of the Sten Scale (i.e., either a 1 or 10) will represent a small percentage (2.5%) of the general population.

Figure 3. Bell Curve

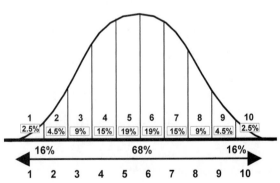

The TotalView Assessment assesses four General Ability scales, three Interest scales, twelve Personality scales, and a Social Desirability scale. The TotalView Assessment test booklet contains 240 items and is completed by most people in less than 60 minutes. The TotalView Assessment Report contains descriptions of the characteristics of the person being evaluated based on the above scales.

The TotalView Assessment Report tells how quickly people learn. It also indicates whether a person has a desire to work with people, data, and things and gives an evaluation of key personality characteristics that affect job performance.

The integrity of the TotalView Assessment Report is verified by four built-in self-validation methods. This makes the TotalView Assessment resistant to attempts to "fake it" or manipulate the results.

To receive additional information on the TotalView, or to take a complimentary assessment, visit:

www.totalviewassessments.com

To discuss how the TotalView Assessment can improve your current selection, deployment, and retention efforts, call 1-800-822-2801, ext. 161 to speak with one of our associates.

References

Adler, Lou. *Hire With Your Head: A Rational Way to Make a Gut Decision.* John Wiley & Sons, Inc.: New York. 1998.

Chiron, Robert J., Fear, Richard A. *The Evaluation Interview.* Fourth Edition. McGraw-Hill: New York. 1990.

Deems, Richard S. *Interviewing: More Than a Gut Feeling.* American Media Publishing: Iowa. 1994.

Hartley, Darin E. *Job Analysis at the Speed of Reality.* HRD Press, Inc. 1999.

Legal Information Institute. Cornell Law School.

Levinstein, Bob. President and C.O.O. of NationJob. Personal Interview, 2/21/01.

Pinsker, Richard J. *Hiring Winners: Profile, Interview, Evaluate.* AMACOM: New York. 1991.

Walsh, Mary Williams. "Luring the Best in an Unsettled Time." *The NewYork Times,* January 30, 2001.

Index

About the Author

Sarah J. Ennis has spent numerous years research-
ing, designing, and conducting training programs to
help organizations and their employees learn and
grow. Sarah has designed programs that are being
used nationally and internationally on subjects
ranging from management and leadership to communication and customer service. She resides in
Iowa where she researches, writes, and conducts
corporate and public presentations. You can e-mail
Sarah at www.sarahennis@qwest.net.